A Step
at a Time

The Autobiography of the World-Renowned Health Guru

Jan de Vries

MAINSTREAM
PUBLISHING

EDINBURGH AND LONDON

First published in Great Britain in 2002 by
MAINSTREAM PUBLISHING COMPANY (EDINBURGH) LTD
7 Albany Street
Edinburgh EH1 3UG

ISBN 1 84018 656 9

A catalogue record for this book is available from the British Library

Typeset in Ehrhardt and Footlight
Printed and bound in Great Britain by
Creative Print Design Wales

Contents

Foreword

You will treasure this book. The life of Jan de Vries is enthralling. More importantly, his philosophy of life and healing are of the utmost value.

Jan de Vries was born in a small Dutch town in 1937. Under the Nazi occupation, he helped his mother find food for people she was hiding. Little Jan ran horrific risks; he still carries the mark of an explosion and he has a couple of squint fingers because his hands were frozen as he waited for hours in a queue for prunes for his grandmother. At one point in this hell, the child prayed that if his mother and he were saved, he would care about the well-being of people for the rest of his life.

Jan gained his degree when he was 21. He continued to pursue a special interest in pharmacy. In 1958 he was in Amsterdam, and he happened to go to a lecture that touched on homoeopathy.

'What do you think?' asked the man in the next seat.

'This is for spinsters and old wives,' said Jan.

'You must have a very small mind,' came the reply.

This was one of those moments that can galvanise and

define a life. The man in the next seat was Dr Alfred Vogel, the great authority on herbs, natural healing and homoeopathy. Jan's heart and instincts, despite what he had said to Vogel, were passionately against the small-minded, and this passion is part of Jan's creative life force today as much as when he was a student. Jan went on to study osteopathy in Germany and Holland. He managed to get into China, where he studied acupuncture. He worked in Taiwan. All his life, he has explored different modes of healing. He also worked with Dr Vogel, who had challenged him at the lecture; indeed, Jan became the only pupil whom Vogel 'really taught'.

Some 40 years after the lecture in Amsterdam, Jan de Vries was in London. He made time in a crowded schedule for a stranger who had no appointment. That stranger was me. I had just been diagnosed with a malignant cancer of which a textbook writes that 'the median survival time is under a year in untreated patients, and two to three years with treatment'. I was in despair. But I happened to read Jan de Vries's book, *Cancer and Leukaemia*, and its account of an elaborate Chinese breathing exercise with visualisations. I tried the exercise and had a hunch that it was helping me. So I tracked down Dr de Vries.

I describe the meeting in my book, *Living Proof: A Medical Mutiny*:

> When my turn comes to see him, de Vries writes notes, as if there is not a second to spare, but he scarcely looks at the pad.
>
> His eyes focus on mine.
>
> For a whole minute.
>
> Perhaps more.
>
> I can hear his pen scratching, otherwise we might be

anywhere. Then there is a shutdown of his
concentration and he writes a prescription.

'One look at you, and you do not need chemotherapy.'

I am so surprised that I do not ask why. Dr de
Vries's extra-sensory minute, if it was that, is over. He
is recharging his energy for the next patient . . .

'You can sort out this melanoma. Goodbye.'

At the time of this meeting with Jan, five cancer specialists,
independently of each other, were urging me to start
chemotherapy: if I did not, they said, the probability was that
I would be dead in a year. But I decided to follow the contrary
advice of Jan. I felt, by instinct, that something radical had
occurred during our meeting, an inner world had been pierced
– I write about it further in *Living Proof: A Medical Mutiny*.
Jan also prescribed potassium drops (to help alkalise the body)
and endorsed the Chinese breathing exercises and nutritional
therapies which I was starting to follow.

Eight years on, I still have not had chemotherapy or
radiotherapy. And I continue to do my job.

Living Proof: A Medical Mutiny, was published in March
2002. Jan read it and was astonished when he came to my
account of our meeting because he discovered that I am the
first patient, to his knowledge, to suspect that he has an extra
sense of intuition that assists him in his work.

So this was another chance meeting that produced great
results. Jan's generosity in 1994, when he fitted in a stranger
with no appointment, helped to save my life, just as he helped
his mother – although in a different way – to save lives when
he was a boy under the Nazis. Also, *Living Proof* sparked off
this magnificent autobiography by Jan, *A Step at a Time*.

A Step at a Time reveals that Jan became aware as a boy,

at the age of about four or five, of his extra-sensory gifts. Yet, as I read his pages, I also think of the parable of the talents in Matthew 25. Jan was accorded a gift, but he turned it into an achievement. He treasured God's blessing but he also studied pharmacy, osteopathy, acupuncture, herbalism and many other approaches to healing. Like the good servants in Matthew, he laboured with hard work and humility to double the talent he was given. 'Well done, thou good and faithful servant,' says the Lord when he returns from the far country where he had travelled. And he also says to the servants who had worked, 'Enter thou into the joy of the Lord.'

Jan's sense of joy in life was clear to me even in his hurried consultation over my cancer. His joy was a presence, a psychic reality, a catalyst for healing, an unspoken celebration. I wrote at the time that 'de Vries is generous', as in one of my favourite texts: 'So let him give, not grudgingly or of necessity, for God loveth a cheerful giver.' (2 Corinthians 9:7) It is a quality you will find on every page of *A Step at a Time*.

Jan was a turning point in my own struggle with cancer, and I can try to state his philosophy by linking him with my next turning point, the senior Professor of Medicine in the University of Oxford, Sir David Weatherall FRS. In *Living Proof*, I describe how I sat in the Institute of Molecular Medicine, a world centre of advanced research, and told Sir David about Jan and the various therapies of diet and visualisation that I followed.

> 'Do you think I am mad to try what I am doing?' I ask.
>
> Sir David Weatherall is a man who thinks for as long as he wishes before he speaks. A minute or two pass.
>
> 'What you must understand, Mr Gearin-Tosh, is that we know so little about how the body works.'

I am astonished.

Sir David repeats his remark.

'We know so little about how the body works.'

Nine short words.

It is in the context of these nine short words that doctors of vision, dedication and humility are so crucial. Jan pleads in *A Step at a Time* for so-called orthodox and complementary medicine to work together. He aptly quotes the biblical expression 'where there is no vision, the people perish' (Proverbs 29:18). Sir David wrote for *Living Proof*, 'Though I do believe passionately in scientific medicine, I have not got to the stage of being so blinkered that I cannot believe that at least some aspects of the more complementary approach to medicine may have a lot to offer. I think they could be put to scientific test, and should be, but whether this will happen is far from clear.'

Mankind has always needed men and women of vision who step ahead of their time and who have the courage to do so. *A Step at a Time* is Jan's wise, proportionate and modest title. But its inner meaning is that of Sir David Weatherall: a step *ahead* of time. A step ahead of mere convention. A step, certainly, ahead of small-mindedness, the peril which Dr Vogel articulated to Jan almost half a century ago at that lecture in Amsterdam. A step that leads into the unknown. A step that others should follow.

Steps that lead forward have never been more necessary than they are today. They are the value and joy of Jan's life and of *A Step at a Time*.

Michael Gearin-Tosh,
St Catherine's College,
University of Oxford.

Preface

Sitting in front of a Jan de Vries seminar, I felt very much part of the lecture . . . but not part of the audience! Leaving my possessions lying on the seat, I crept three-quarters of the way down the side of the hall and stood unobtrusively in the shadows, quietly scanning the silent, intent faces. I became more involved with the audience than with the lecture. I saw and felt earnest and eager anticipation, the wonder of enlightenment, great hope for the future, pleading in the faces of the sick, renewed energy in the faces of the not so sick, a restoring of their love for humankind. Not a shuffle, not a cough – Jan de Vries was once more spreading the word of natural love and harmony!

Through his work and lecture tours, Jan de Vries is fast becoming recognised in the West as one of the leading pioneers in the holistic and alternative approach to medicine. When he brought naturopathy to Britain 35 years ago, it was virtually unknown, although other countries throughout the world had been using these methods for centuries. How was it that we in the West managed to forget, ignore and totally

dismiss these wonderful natural and effective methods? We desperately needed pioneers like Jan de Vries to bring us back to our senses, to help us recognise the damage we had done, particularly since the Industrial Revolution.

Despite his great success and many achievements, Jan still manages to convey a sense of simplicity. He is always willing to talk to anyone with a question, whatever the question. He is always approachable on the telephone. Even during one of his increasingly sought-after clinic sessions, he will allow himself to be interrupted.

I have studied his books, listened to his radio broadcasts and followed his journeys across the continent, and have come to realise that this man's main message to us all is very simple – it is love. Jan de Vries believes that true love is the body and soul's finest and most exacting natural cure of all.

Diane Hemmings –
Patient and Holistic Medical Therapist,
co-founder of the Healing Hands Network.

ℜ CHAPTER ONE ℜ

Second Fiddle to the Ironing Board

On a wintry, snowy day in January 1937 (and in Holland winter can be very, very cold), my mother started a chore that she had hated all her life but, nevertheless, always did herself – ironing! This was a job she really loathed, and in the company of a pound of cherry chocolates perched on the end of the ironing board, she tried to get through the pile of clothes as quickly as possible. However, right in the middle of this, she realised that she was going into labour. She sent my brother Nicolas, who was 13 at the time, to ask the local midwife (who lived just round the corner) to come. She hurried immediately to the house and not long after, at ten past four in the afternoon, I was born. (At that time in Holland, babies were always born at home.) There, by the River IJssel, which was completely frozen, in Voorstraat 51, a very healthy boy arrived. My mother's friend came in to help and, as soon as she got things settled, she left and walked up to my father's factory to tell him that he was richer by one son.

I was wanted very much by my mother when I was born, but a great disappointment to my father, because he had wanted a daughter. He was making his way home from work

15

when my mother's friend met him in the street and told him the wonderful news. He was so disappointed that he went back to the factory straight away.

My father was very set in his ways and, although he was a proper gentleman, he lived in his own world, dominated by music and religion. My mother, who had a very friendly, gentle character, coped with my father's ways. Nevertheless, she had to take the lead. She was a great personality and I was very close to her as I grew up. My mother was also a very hard-working woman, whilst my father went at a slower pace.

The little place in which I was born, Kampen, had a tremendous history. Although my father's profession – cigar-making – was the main industry of the area, enamel pots and pans were also manufactured, and agriculture played an important part too, being carried on from one generation to the next. Several large buildings – for instance, the local council hall and the church (which was almost as big as a cathedral) – dominated the town. There was a lot of life in that little place as people busied themselves with their merchandise. It was also a very close community. The people of Kampen are fiercely loyal to each other. Even today, if an outsider criticises a Kampenaar to another local, they will loyally defend them.

The IJssel was very busy with ships going up and down the river. Money was spent on treasures that were housed in the old council hall and the church, thus helping to preserve the past for future generations, giving a picture of what life was like for their ancestors. Some very valuable pieces are still there today which show that, at the time, Kampen was one of the richest Hanze cities. The cigar industry was widespread and I remember well the hundreds and hundreds of cigar-makers who ensured that they produced the very best – even the cigars that Churchill smoked were made in our little town.

A number of very famous people were born in this town, including Professor Kolf, who invented the kidney dialysis machine in the 1940s, and whom I will talk more about later. It was well known for its two theological universities. Religion caused a lot of strife in the town and, although largely Protestant, there were large groups of many different religious bodies in Kampen. At one time, standing on a bridge in the town, you could count 12 different places of worship and I don't know how many manses for ministers and lay preachers. There were many divisions, and conflict about moral issues, right and wrong, dominated people's thoughts. Perhaps that was the reason I began to question these things later on in life.

A military high school was located in the town, and some of my uncles (who were military officers) underwent training there. It became a very famous school as, even before the war, Germany sent soldiers there for training. Overall, our little town was booming and it certainly had a lot of positive energy.

My family's roots were there. Many generations, both from my father's and mother's side, were born and brought up in Kampen, and they had a great influence on its history. The IJssel, stemming from the Rhine, was a great river for sailing along. I remember my father and I sailing there, enjoying the beauty of the scenery and the town.

My father was the product of a Jewish family from the beautiful town of Amsterdam. Although in her day it was somewhat unusual, my grandmother had married a much younger man; she was very good-looking. I remember her as a very kind-hearted person and, if we went to visit her on a Saturday, she would give us one or two pennies to make sure that we had enough money to buy some apples or other fruit when we returned – she didn't like us to buy sweets. It was always a delight to visit my grandmother and see my

grandfather smoking his very long pipe in the cosy atmosphere of their home. My grandfather on my mother's side was in the cigar industry, and my grandmother was a great source of information. We loved to go and visit her and, later on in life, although she was nearly blind and we were grown up, she was still of tremendous help in answering any questions we had about our youth, as she was a fount of information. I used to kneel on the floor, listening to her for hours, as she was also a wonderful storyteller. She told us all about the little town where I was born, and its rich history. She had a tremendous interest in military life and, because all her sons were in the army, she hoped that they would become military men of courage. She was a wonderful cook too and we often enjoyed sumptuous meals with her.

I feel privileged to have been born in Kampen, which had a charm and vibrancy that is still very evident today, and I am always happy to return. However, not long after I was born, dark clouds slowly came over Holland as the Second World War loomed. It was not an easy world in which to grow up.

❧ CHAPTER TWO ❧

Batten Down the Hatches

The war started and misery was everywhere. Food was very restricted and the nights were dark, with no lights. People had no idea what was happening and I was too young to understand what was going on. However, as the war began to take its toll, I also came to experience the unhappiness that everybody was talking about. My father and brother were taken away by the Germans and deported. First of all, my father was sent to Apeldoorn in Holland and then Nicolas, my brother, was deported to Germany.

My mother, being kind-hearted, helped everybody around her and had a lot of people in danger from the Nazis staying in the house, even hiding them under the floorboards when she knew the Germans were after them. She was quite a forceful woman and, as she was very much against the Nazi regime, people from all sides turned to her for help. In her own quiet way, she worked tirelessly to ensure people's safety and played an important role in providing a safe shelter – not only in the short term, but sometimes also for longer periods.

Because I was very young – still only eight when the war ended – and could easily walk along the streets without causing

suspicion, I was able to help in many ways and worked very hard to assist my mother. My mother knew of various sources she could rely on to obtain some food for the people she was hiding. One day, she told me to go to a certain farm – no questions asked, I was just told to do it. I was informed that the farmer would be waiting for me with his hay cart and I was to direct him to our house. It is quite interesting to note that farms were very often located in the middle of our town and shelter was provided for the cattle in the backs of houses. People were accustomed to seeing hay being hauled up and put through upstairs windows to be used for feeding the animals. This was very much the done thing in those days, so a farmer with a full load of hay going through the streets was a common sight. The particular farmer I was sent to meet had a cart laden with hay, pulled by two horses. However, unknown to me, a Jewish girl was hiding among the hay and had to be transported to our house, where she remained in safety for quite some time. I never realised at that time that I was actually helping with the underground work, but in so doing I saved this girl's life, because she managed to survive the war without being caught. My mother took situations like this in her stride and we luckily managed to get enough food for the people living with us.

Food was hard to come by. As I mentioned earlier, my father was in the tobacco industry and a lot of people knew him. So, at around the age of five, I was frequently sent to try and get some milk from the nearby farms so that my mother could feed the people she was hiding. The farmers knew my father well and I was often lucky enough to get some milk from them, but it was a very, very sad time.

Two things happened during the Second World War that made me determined to help others. At the age of about four

or five, I remember very clearly going with my mother one Sunday afternoon to visit an uncle of hers (a brother of my grandmother). I always loved to visit my great-uncles because they were very good musicians and all of them could play an instrument of some sort. It was marvellous to hear them playing the flute, the violin and the trumpet. In their time, these men were very well known as musicians. Sadly, the uncle we had gone to visit that day was quite ill and, while I was at his house, something happened which has stayed with me all my life. Because I had never visited a seriously ill person before, I was surprised when a very bitter taste suddenly came into my mouth, and I had to ask my mother if we could leave as I thought I was going to be sick. I was not actually sick at all, but the bitter taste remained in my mouth until we had returned home. The next day, my great-uncle died.

Later in life, I realised that a bitter taste always appears in my mouth when somebody is dying. I really didn't understand its significance at first, but then I noticed that, wherever we were, if there was somebody there who was very ill and I got this taste in my mouth, then usually the next day that person would die. It is a great gift, because if I meet patients and am uncertain about their health, but get that taste in my mouth, I always send them immediately to their doctor or the hospital. Very often, I have not even needed to examine these patients or manipulate them in any way, because I knew that they were very seriously ill. This particular phenomenon has stayed with me throughout my life.

Another very peculiar thing happened during the winter of 1944. At that time, we often had to live in darkness. When there was a threat of bombardment, we were naturally completely cut off from electricity. In addition to this, our windows had to be covered with thick black paper during the

black-out so that no light was visible from the houses. We had no candles to provide us with light. We did, however, have a little windmill at home, which helped a bit with this problem. During air raids we were locked in underground shelters. I noticed that when I was sitting across from people, if it was pitch dark, I could see colours around them. Later on in life, when I learned that everybody has an aura, I realised that was what I could see. Occasionally some people can see these colours. When I learned about Kirlian photography (which can be used to photograph auras), I realised that this was not so odd, but a science that existed, although auras are not seen by everybody. I was aware that these things were gifts that God had entrusted to me, which I could use in the future to benefit others. My perception of things became so strong that usually I could intuitively tell my mother when there was danger around.

Because I was very underweight and, as the doctor had told my mother, completely undernourished, I became quite nervous. As a result of this nervous condition, I often became uncontrollable and difficult to handle. In fact, I was always looking for something to do, as I got bored very quickly. I realised what the Germans were capable of, though, and knew very well that I could not do anything wrong or they would shoot me. I became more aware of this when I heard of acquaintances of my mother's who were shot because of their underground work in the Resistance. My mother had to be very careful of the dangers involved when protecting others against the enemy.

One day, I put the whole town under tremendous stress. My

mother, who was trying to get coupons for the many people she was looking after, was standing in a queue at the distribution office. As my father's youngest brother was a civil servant and in charge of distributing these coupons, I knew that he would help my mother to the best of his ability. Naturally, after a while of waiting in the queue, I got very bored. I noticed a bell quite high up by a ronepipe and, to relieve my boredom, quickly climbed up the pipe and pressed the bell. It turned out to be an air raid alarm and the whole town was thrown into a state of panic. The Germans were raging and everybody was greatly distressed. My uncle, I remember, came out of his office, shouting about what could have happened. They knew that as the alarm had gone off from that distribution office, somebody must have touched the bell. Until today, nobody ever found out who did it because I was like quicksilver, and speedily hid myself under my mother's big raincoat! The newspapers reported the alarm but, as nobody knew who had set it off, luckily I escaped notice.

That was the sort of thing I got up to and my mother, I am sure, had quite a job keeping me under control. When it came to pestering the Germans, I was always number one, because I really hated them, knowing how much harm they were doing to our town and its people. Usually, when they marched along the street, as boys we would yell at them, singing '*Tom Tom kijk eens om, kijk eens naar beneden. Kijk eens naar die grote stad. Heel Berlin is plat.*' The words meant that when the English (Tommies) flew over our town, they were to look down, see what the Germans had done and then go and flatten Berlin. This made the Germans absolutely furious and usually we had to run away very quickly, otherwise they would have shot us. At the beginning of the war they were not so vicious, but as the war heightened they became more and more frightening.

Food was always in short supply. I remember once, when we were very hungry, I heard that a greengrocer had prunes. I had never seen a prune in all my life but stood the whole day in the fierce cold waiting in a queue to get some as a surprise for my grandmother. After standing there all morning and afternoon, at seven o'clock at night, I was so disappointed when the greengrocer's wife told all the people who had been waiting patiently in the cold that her husband hadn't come back, so there would be no prunes for them. When I went to my grandmother's house, she noticed that both my little fingers were almost frozen and managed to save them, although they have been squint ever since. If anybody asks me why I don't have straight pinkies, I explain to them that it happened during the war.

The war kept raging on. Things became more and more difficult and many Dutch people were half-starved. Schooling was almost impossible. My school was taken over by the Germans and used as a pigsty, so it became redundant. In the midst of all this turmoil, there was a little bright point. On a very wintry day, during an air raid, my little sister was born. I knew there was something going on as I was put out of the house. A short time later, I heard that I had a little sister, which would have delighted my father but, by this time, he had been taken away by the Germans, together with my brother. I can still remember to this day the posters that were put up on noticeboards throughout the town decreeing that all men under the age of 65 had to enlist with the Germans, either in Holland or in Germany. Although a lot of men were deported to Germany, many remained in Holland. However, those who did not enlist ran the risk of being picked up and classed as an anti-Nazi. The difficult part was recognising betrayers, as you never knew who they were. They would then

report you to the Germans for not having signed up and these people were then caught and deported, like my father and brother – some of them had to endure great hardship.

Everybody was delighted by the birth of my sister, until clouds gathered over that happiness. The doctor who was in charge of the birth found that she had been born with a cancerous tumour on her back. My mother, being as strong as ever, arranged a meeting that morning, took things in hand and said to the doctor that she would try and get some advice from Professor Kolf, a well-known surgeon and the inventor of the artificial kidney machine, now known as kidney dialysis. He examined my sister and told my mother that the tumour had been caused by an unbalanced food pattern – the result, in other words, of the limited variety of food available during the war. This had made our diet very one-sided. I often thought later that he was one of the first orthodox doctors who recognised how important food was in relation to good health, and that unbalanced food patterns can cause problems and possibly disease.

Our doctor and Professor Kolf decided that my sister would have to go to nearby Zwolle for treatment. Unfortunately, the doctor sympathised with the Germans but, fortunately for my mother, he managed to get transport to take my sister there, where she became the first person in the world to receive radium treatment, which was successful. My sister was saved, and is still alive and kicking.

After the birth of my sister, when things got back to normal a bit, I had more and more free time and was usually quick to get into mischief. One day I had a tremendous shock when some boys and I were searching for food. I remember being very hungry, because I had been sitting on the refuse heap at the local milk factory all morning looking for little pieces of

black coal that had not been burned, so that I could give these to my poor old grandmother. I sat there for many hours and came home with no more than a pound of little pieces of black coal. In the afternoon, we went around rooting for food and I remember, as so often happened, that I had been eating grass to keep my rumbling tummy quiet. During our search, we came across an enormous car, full of food. I was amazed at what was in that car and had never seen the likes of it before – there were tins and packets, sugar and butter of unknown quantity. It was like paradise, and not a German in sight. Because I was small and very quick, I went into the car and started to throw out the food. After a while, planes came over and started to shoot at the car. Our lives were really in danger at that moment, and we crawled to the river where we hid ourselves in the rushes, terrified that they would find us and we would be shot. That experience left me with a small dent in my head where one of the grenade pieces hit it but I was lucky because it did not do any real damage. Amazingly, that was the only physical war wound I received. Often when people make fun of alternative medicine, I say to them, 'This is one of the reasons I have a hole in my head' and let them feel the dent on top of my skull.

There were many great miracles in the Second World War, and one I shall never forget happened very late one night. At the time my mother was hiding quite a number of people in the house. The doorbell rang and I awakened to hear my mother going to the door. There stood a man wearing one clog and one normal shoe. He took a piece of paper out of his pocket and said to my mother that he had been given her address as a safe place to go to, and could he please come in as he had escaped from a ship which was taking him to a concentration camp. My mother let him in. He had scabies

from top to toe, but she covered him with ichthyol ointment, which is still used today for scabies. It was lucky that she dealt with the man so quickly, because my aunt came over to warn my mother of a commotion in the street. The Germans were looking for a man who had escaped. My mother hid him under the floorboards, where he joined the other people already hiding there, and said to me, 'Now we have to go down on our knees and pray very hard that God will save us.' The Germans were going around like lions turning over every house from top to bottom. Then the miracle happened. Although they turned over every other house, they never even touched our front door – one of the real miracles that I experienced during the war.

Not long after, my mother was asked to go to Arnhem Oosterbeek to help out in a home for elderly people. Although there were people in our home being hidden from the Germans, my mother was needed there, so we had to go. We went to Arnhem Oosterbeek, where my mother's friend was the assistant matron; she also played a role in the work of the Resistance.

This brought about a turning point in my life. Again, there was no school there for me to attend, but next to the house was a big monastery which housed a lot of monks, and I got friendly with one of them. He played a great part in my young life. I must have been intelligent enough to take in what he said as he taught me a lot and made a very big impression on me. Although I was only very young, while we stayed there I went to help him in the herb garden every day. He told me all about herbs and plants, roots and trees, and what they were used for. With great passion, he taught me of God's creation and the wonders of nature. This instilled in me a great love for man and nature.

I still remember how heartbreaking it was when my mother came one day and said that we had to move, and fast. I never saw a place empty so quickly as then, which was very sad, but right under the eyes of the Germans everybody was led to safety for another day. Hitler bombarded Oosterbeek nearly to the ground. The house we had been living in was completely flattened. I remember a little friend, who was really good to me and still is. She and I were allowed, after these great bombardments, to see the damage. The death and destruction that the Nazis had wreaked was overwhelming. With my instilled love for God and Creation, I could not understand why this was happening. That same day I promised God that if my mother and I were saved from this terrible hell, I would care about the well-being of people for the rest of my life. I hope I have kept that promise in the many years I have devoted to helping people and I will continue to do so until my dying day – I want to fulfil that promise to do what I can to help the less privileged, not only in this country but in others as well, and especially in the Third World.

The war raged on, but Hitler was losing ground. Finally, on 17 April 1945, our little town of Kampen was liberated by the Canadian and Scots troops. I can still picture them coming in their jeeps. That was the first time in my life that I had seen chocolate. When I was given some by one of the soldiers I took it home and showed it to my mother! She broke off a little piece and said 'Taste it!' I told my mother how wonderful it was and she said to me, 'Respect it all your life and never eat too much of it.' Nowadays, when I see the half- or one-metre bars of chocolate people buy, I still get shocked.

I remember my father came back from Germany in very poor health, his arms and legs thinner than a baby's. However, my mother fed him up as best she could from the little food

we had and he survived. Every day, I went onto the street to watch people arriving back from concentration camps and places they had been hiding, and every day I looked to see if my brother was amongst them. Every day, I returned home without my brother and saw my mother crying in the hope that one day he would return. Finally, when he did come home, holding a bundle of coupons in his hand, he looked as if there had never been a war. He told my mother that he had been to every distribution office, telling them that he had just come back from Germany and needed coupons. He told my mother that we could have a big party now, as we had plenty of coupons.

He had been very lucky. Because he had told the Germans that he was a first-class cook, he landed work in the kitchen. Uppermost in his mind at that time was that he had to be able to eat if he was to survive his time in Germany, so he ended up in the best place.

I remember the marvellous party there was after we were all reunited and the war was over. The whole Dutch nation was full of promise – everybody wanted a united Holland, with one religion, one political party and the guarantee that there would never be a war again. People were so thankful that the war had ended that there was much harmony and togetherness. When I think of those parties and the wonderful festivities we had at that time, and the religious battles that Holland has had over the years and the tremendous number of political parties now, it is clear that those promises have long been forgotten. Holland is more divided now than it ever was before the Second World War.

When I see how people take food for granted and their disrespect for it, I still remember the days when we would have been so happy just to have a crumb to eat. Nowadays

people throw away good food with no gratitude for what they have been given and no thought of the many people in the world suffering from hunger, who would give anything for that food. Important lessons have to be learned.

I suppose that my experiences during the war, of which I have given only a few examples in this chapter, taught me to respect life and to fight for it. Life is very valuable. When I look around and see how life is taken for granted in many people's eyes, I am often reminded of those days when life was so precious and how many people were cut down in their prime by the Nazi monsters. As the war progressed, things got so difficult that people started to eat tulip bulbs – and even their own dogs and cats – because they were so hungry. Luckily, by this stage the war was coming to an end.

Before it ended, however, something happened which would determine my future. It was an accident which took place towards the end of 1943. I never would have thought then, because of that accident, I would end up spending most of my life in Britain. I must have been about seven years of age when we saw a bomber on fire going down over our town. The plane took a nosedive into the beautiful IJssel. When the bodies were dredged from the water, I saw the full horror: the six military men in the plane, who had been transporting bombs, had been shot down by the Germans and lost their lives. They were buried in the nearby cemetery and, after some time, I was asked to look after the grave of the navigator, Charlie Young. His full title was Flying Officer C.W.R. Young, Air Bomber, Royal Air Force, who died 13 June 1943, aged 27. I did this faithfully, and every Sunday went up to the cemetery, taking some flowers with me. With great devotion, I took this job upon myself and looked after that grave with great care. There were simple, little crosses upon each grave, and flowers on

each one. Later on, proper gravestones replaced these crosses, very nicely done and all in keeping with each other. The inscriptions on each grave read 'Sunshine and shadows by turn but always love', which reminded me of other young people who had lost their lives in their fight for freedom during that war.

Years later, I understood much better than I ever could as a child the words from the Bible: 'It is not in man that walketh to direct his steps.' (Jeremiah 10:23) Later it would become quite clear why this job had been entrusted to me.

Now that the war was over, I had to restart my education, which was very difficult. It wasn't easy to get me to attend school because I simply hated it. However, although I'd had broken years at kindergarten and the first classes of school (I missed primary two to primary four almost entirely), I was determined to work hard and make up for lost time. I really had to discipline myself to make up for those wasted years.

❧ CHAPTER THREE ❧

The Reluctant Scholar

By the time the war was over, I dreaded the thought of going back to school. My past experience of school made me almost hate it. I had also become used to a certain measure of freedom during the war. In Holland, education is very different to Britain. There are religious schools with biblical lessons and non-religious schools. My father was a very strict, religious man, and before the war he insisted that I go to the Christian school for infants, where they put great emphasis on the Bible. Because I was too young to understand what this was all about, I went to school quite happily at first. I attended a small school on the Ebbinge Straat. The schoolmistress there was Miss Aman. I just loved Miss Aman – she really impressed me. She had a very old-fashioned hairstyle and looked lovely. She was also a good storyteller and in the morning I loved to listen to her as she told us stories from the Bible – until somebody in our neighbourhood died and I heard people saying that he was going to heaven. Miss Aman used to tell us all sorts of wonderful stories from the Bible and about people going to heaven or to hell, so I was very intrigued by the whole subject. Being inquisitive, this led me to ask

questions, and I kept asking questions until one day Miss Aman went to see my father and mother and told them that it would probably be better if I went to a school where they did not teach the bible as she felt that the bible stories were really troubling me, and that the questions I kept asking were really not suitable for the other children to hear.

I was moved to another school where the headmistress was called Miss de Groot. She was a much stricter headmistress and it was a much bigger school but, nevertheless, I loved to go to this school with my cousins in the Panjansteeg. I went faithfully and quite enjoyed my time there until the Germans took the building over and the school had to be closed. By that time, I had managed to learn a little bit from primary one. My father then wanted me to go to another religious school. I did quite well there and my new teacher, Miss Nip, was quite understanding but, again, my questions about the bible came to the fore. She decided to talk to me at lunchtime and made such an impression on me that we remained friends all our lives. Suddenly, that school was taken over by the Germans to be used as a pigsty so, basically, from primary two until primary four, I received no formal education apart from an occasional day here and there in a church or in a hall, but it was so sporadic that I had to have extra teaching at home.

Back in primary four, after the war we all had to work very hard to make up for lost time. The Julianna School had quite a few good teachers then and Miss van Dyk was especially kind to me. She often came to school in a horse and carriage and bribed me by saying that if I was extremely good and obedient she would take me home in her horse and carriage, as she lived near me. This was, of course, a very exciting experience and I enjoyed it so much that I started to love school, until a gentleman teacher replaced Miss van Dyk. He was very strict

and realised that I had a lot to learn so, of course, I began to hate school again. Nevertheless, I had no choice but to get on with it as I realised my mother was monitoring the whole situation. One day I went home with a bad report and I will never forget how terribly angry she was. The mark I had received for behaviour was very low. At that time, my father was still in Germany, where he had been deported.

The headmaster took the next class I went into. He was a real tyrant and, at one point, I remember only too well that when he talked about the Church, history or religion, he spoke at great length about Roman Catholics and how they had tortured the Protestants. I said in the class that I had also read of the followers of Calvin and Zwingli burning Catholics alive. This made him very angry and my punishment was to sit and work on my own in one of the classrooms for two weeks. He asked how I dared criticise the great reformers. Until this day, I still don't understand the behaviour of that headmaster as I knew only too well, even as a young boy, that when two people fight both are at fault. By that time I had started to form my own opinions on religion, being from a Protestant family on my father's side and a Catholic family on my mother's. After forming my own opinion on the whole matter, I decided to talk to the assistant headmaster who had taken my class in primary six and was a wonderful person. His name was Mr Nijboer. He had a great influence on my life and I still regard him as a great philosopher and a most understanding teacher. With a lot of encouragement, he helped me and, again, I became very friendly with him. He had a small farm, where I was always made very welcome on my free days, and where he gave me a lot of private tuition to improve my levels at school. Although the headmaster had told him not to waste his time on me because I would never amount to anything and would be of no

use to society, Mr Nijboer worked hard to prove him wrong and he certainly succeeded. He was very patient with me and, to this day, I am grateful for the contribution he made during my formative years.

Now that the first part of my education had finished, I had to go to secondary school. Here again, my impatient nature got the better of me and the headmaster had great problems with me, especially as he was influenced by the headmaster of my previous school. He was advised not to waste time on me and just to let me 'get on with things'.

Although I hated going to school, there were certain subjects I worked very hard at. Believe it or not, I was top of my class for poetry, singing and drama and was awarded first prize in most competitions. This made me feel as if I was somebody important. Luckily, experience soon knocked that out of me.

On one special evening, when almost the whole town was present, I was assigned three very special roles – the first of these was to sing on my own, the second was to play the main role in a short drama and the third was to recite a beautiful piece of poetry. The singing went perfectly, as did the drama. Finally came the piece of poetry. I recalled often seeing my father looking very intently at his watch while holding a meeting. While standing on the platform, I made the big mistake of copying my father by looking at my watch before starting to recite the poetry. That was frowned on in those days, and the audience all booed me. The next day, the local papers said how wonderful my singing and acting had been, but I got no sympathy when it came to the poetry as it was felt I had been too big for my boots! I also had to face my mother, who humbled me in such a way that I lost my confidence. The entire experience affected me to such an extent that it took a long time before my self-confidence

returned and, even now, I catch a glimpse of this at times when I am lecturing in front of very large audiences, especially in the United States where I often come face-to-face with thousands of people. Nevertheless, I gained one thing from that experience which I have kept at the forefront of my mind all my life, and that is to remain humble, think of the simple things in life and never boast. Boasting is something that I hate hearing, which is probably due to the fact that I tried too hard in my younger days to impress people, but my own stupidity on the platform that evening brought me back down to earth.

Despite the many punishments I received for being naughty – which often led to the headmaster calling on my parents to complain – I still managed to progress through my school years.

Fortunately, I managed to find a lot of work outside school because I felt there was more to life than just homework and hanging about. By pure luck, one day I stepped into a bookshop and asked the owner if he could give me some work on Saturdays or in the evenings as I wanted to make a few pennies. Mr de Jong said he would think about it and asked me to go back the next day. I met his wife and I think she must have liked me, because I was offered the job of keeping his library of books in order, which I did with great enthusiasm.

This couple had a lot of business interests, including a printing company and, without my realising it, Mr de Jong was gradually familiarising me in all matters relating to his businesses. He even brought me to the printing company, where one of the foremen taught me all about printing. I had a whale of a time and decided I wanted to leave school as soon as possible. Of course, this was out of the question, as my parents would not allow it. Undeterred, one evening Mr and

Mrs de Jong came to my parents' home and pleaded – especially with my mother – to permit them to train me in all aspects of their businesses, as they had no children of their own and felt I would be the perfect person to take over the running of their businesses one day. They added that they wanted to educate me in order to prepare me for this responsible position. Somehow, I felt that I could not do this.

However, I enjoyed being with them and loved them dearly. I looked after their dog, did a lot of tidying up for them and even worked late at night window-dressing. One particular occasion made Mr de Jong even more certain that he wanted to keep me in his business. That was on the Queen's birthday. It was a wonderful day and, as one of his shops sold things like lanterns, trumpets, hats and so on, he asked me to go there in the morning to sell these as we had a free day from school. As very little was being sold in the shop, I asked the manageress if I could set up a table outside and take all the goods out on to the street to see if I could sell more that way. By 12 o'clock I had sold the entire stock and when Mr de Jong arrived he was so happy that he hugged me. This convinced him that I was definitely the right person to run his businesses, and he made me a great offer. I felt awful because, in my heart, I realised that my future did not lie in that direction and so I declined all the offers made by Mr and Mrs de Jong. Sadly, following that difficult decision, I felt I could not continue working for them as a bad atmosphere developed.

One morning, on my way to school, I went to collect a little friend from her home. The whole area was blocked off as the house, with 13 people in it, had completely burnt down and was totally in ashes. This was an enormous shock to me and, although I was very young, this tragedy brought me to my senses. At that time, there were strong religious views being

aired regarding this family which I was really too young to understand. There was much religious conflict in my home town and many teachings, due to the presence of the theological universities, and the many different religions that existed in the town. I made up my young mind then (and still believe today) that if you keep to the simplicity of the teachings of Christ, then you cannot go wrong. All thoughts of the reformers and the many people who had their own views on religion went to the back of my mind and I felt that if I could hold on to that belief, things would turn out all right.

I managed to get another good job when I was asked to arrange guided tours of our local church, which was almost as big as a cathedral. I studied the church's history and my guided tours became quite well known. These took place on Saturdays and in the evenings, and the pocket money and gifts that people gave me helped greatly towards my studies. I often had money left over, so I gave this to my mother who then shared it equally with others who were less privileged than us.

There was a pharmacy situated across the road from our house. Somebody new had taken over the business and was rebuilding the whole shop. I took a great interest and, as I knew quite a bit about pharmacy, asked the owner if I could help. The lady who owned the shop was very grateful for any help I could give her. I helped out whenever I could, after attending to the other little jobs I had. Believe it or not, due to our hard work, that particular pharmacy became one of the best in town. The owner encouraged me to study pharmacy and to get a degree in this field, so that I could work for her. The stories she told me about her underground work were absolutely fascinating. I respected this lady for the way in which she had stood up to the Germans as much as she could and, under their very eyes, did so much for the underground

movement. Unfortunately, this took such a toll on her health that she became a very serious diabetic. Many people will remember her as a very bossy lady, but I got on with her well and she helped me a lot when I studied pharmacy which was, in those days, not very easy. In the next chapter, I shall share with you some of my experiences in that pharmacy, where I worked until I graduated.

CHAPTER FOUR

Janny Beuze – 'The Boss'

There I was, totally involved in pharmacy. This was something that my family approved of very much. I had to study extremely hard to obtain my degree and, because I also worked hard at the weekends to build up the pharmacy to be the best in town, it all became too much for me. I had very little time for any private life at all, as I studied and worked hard, but I must say that I got a lot of help from the boss, Janny Beuze. She certainly wasn't easy to work for – in fact, she was very difficult – but I learned then that diabetics were not always the easiest people to deal with. If she wasn't satisfied with something I did, I sometimes had to repeat the job over and over again until I perfected it. She examined any ointment I made in the mortar about ten times before it received her approval. Any other concoctions I made were also very sharply criticised. However, her strict training was instrumental in me becoming a very good pharmacist, and I profited greatly from this experience. I travelled to do my studies and luckily, in July 1958, I got my degree. I remember that I fell down the stairs, with my certificate under my arm, right in the street in Amsterdam. That day eight of us had

gone to sit the exams. In those days they were very difficult, which was emphasised by the fact that of those who sat the exams, only two of us succeeded. I couldn't believe my ears when I heard I had passed. I arrived back in my home town to be greeted by a local fanfare and was treated like a king. Although my head was bursting with knowledge, I had no idea what the future would hold for me but, with the tremendous welcome I received on coming home, I decided that whatever I did, I would try hard to make a good job of it.

About a year later I went to the Krasna Polsky Hotel in Amsterdam to listen to a lecture being given by a German professor on homoeopathy – Professor Zabel – and sat next to an older gentleman. We talked about homoeopathy and when this gentleman asked me what I thought about it, I told him that it was good for old spinsters and old wives. He looked at me and said, 'You must have a very small mind.' That really struck home. I started to talk to him and became very interested in what he had to say. I discovered who he was – Dr Alfred Vogel from Switzerland, a guru of homoeopathic medicine in his time. He told me that he had just come back from a meeting with his best friend, Albert Schweitzer. What he had to say was completely enthralling and I felt that this meeting could open a door for me, so I wanted to keep in contact with him. When I went back to our pharmacy in Kampen, Janny Beuze, who had already made her business into a limited company of which I was a shareholder, was very happy.

When I told my friends about Dr Vogel, nobody was interested. Homoeopathy was taboo in Holland at that time. Nobody wanted to hear about it. Because of the German occupation, anyone involved in homoeopathy had a dirty name as Hitler and Himmler were great followers of it and helped

homoeopathic doctors (those whose allegiance was with the Germans) in Holland during the war in all kinds of ways. Therefore, after the war anybody who had an interest in homoeopathy was looked on as yet another betrayer. When I shared with others the fascinating facts that Dr Vogel had told me about, I lost most of my friends, even my girlfriend, who said this was the quickest route to quackery and I should certainly not get involved in it!

The principles of alternative medicine, however, were very attractive to me and, although I lost most of my friends and became very depressed about that, I wanted to pursue my interest. It was a very lonely battle and I was so down that Janny Beuze suggested I should take a break. This was an ideal opportunity for me to go to Scotland, which I had always wanted to do.

Why Scotland? Remember the plane that was brought down in flames in our town in 1943 and landed in the IJssel, and the navigator's grave I tended with so much care as a child? Well, his family had asked me many times to go over and meet them. So I thought the time was now right as I had always promised them that I would go after I graduated. Never did I think for one minute that my visit to Scotland would bring such an enormous change to my life.

I travelled to Scotland firstly by boat and then by train, and finally arrived in Edinburgh to be met by the father of the dead navigator, Charlie Young. It was a wonderful journey overall and the start of a much-needed break after such a lot of hard work. Before leaving Holland, my aunt handed me a letter and asked if I could deliver it to two ladies who lived in Edinburgh. When we arrived at my host's home, I met Charlie Young's mother and also his widow. She was a lovely lady who had only been married for six weeks when her husband lost his

life in my country. We all had a wonderful time and got on so well together. We became very fond of each other. When I told Mr Young about the letter to be delivered to the two ladies, he said that it was amazing because they lived just up the hill at Royal Terrace, so we could go the following afternoon and deliver it.

When we arrived there the next day, the maid who opened the door said that the ladies were at their sister-in-law's house in Inverleith Place. Mr Young suggested that we deliver the letter to them there. When we arrived at this charming house, the lady who opened the door asked me to come in and introduced me to several people. Unfortunately, my English was very bad. When she asked me when I had arrived in Scotland, I replied, 'I comes tomorrow and here I is.' That was how bad it really was! Out of politeness, they didn't laugh at me but, some time later, we had quite a laugh about it. The ladies who lived in Royal Terrace asked me if I would like to have lunch or dinner with them. I asked my host, who had accompanied me, and it was arranged that I would go to their house for supper on the Sunday evening; this being the most convenient time.

When I arrived on the Sunday night, there were about 26 people already there. While I was sitting talking about Holland (to the best of my ability!), three younger ladies arrived and sat just across from me. One of them especially caught my eye. When we were asked to go through for dinner, I sat across from her. We talked together and I had a great time. Later on in the evening, when it was time to leave, it was decided that the three young ladies would take me. As fate would have it, a car picked up two of the young ladies and I was left alone with the other one.

As she was going in the same direction as me, she said she

would show me the way back to where I was staying. We talked a lot and she impressed me so much that I asked if I could meet her again. So we met again the following Tuesday. By then, I had learned that the lady who had asked me when I had arrived and I had replied, 'I comes tomorrow, here I is,' was the mother of the girl who walked home with me. To cut a long story short, we became very friendly. I invited the family to come to Holland and, when they arrived about six months later, I got engaged to her. She is now my wife and has given me four daughters and ten grandchildren. Another great thing that the war had done for me!

I had the most wonderful time in Scotland and realised then that changes had to be made. This came about when my girlfriend came to Holland and we got engaged, because Janny Beuze became very angry and jealous of my new-found love and things became absolutely impossible between us. She apparently wanted me for herself and did not like the thought that someone else had come along with whom I wanted to share the rest of my life. She was overcome with jealousy, but thought that this relationship with my girlfriend would never last because, as she always said, there is a large sea between Holland and Scotland. She also felt quite secure in the fact that I was close to her, taking care of business matters and, because of the war, I had to carry a lot of responsibility. I certainly could not go on working there and, as I had acquainted myself with Dr Vogel, I decided that I would take up his offer to work with him in Nunspeet and help him establish the first clinic for natural cures in Holland, which soon became one of the best places to go to for health and fitness. This story, however, becomes more interesting in the next chapter.

On my second visit to Edinburgh, I was so amazed at the

splendour of that beautiful city. On one occasion, between Christmas and New Year, I took a bus which, in those days, used to have a conductor on board. As the bus went round a corner, there was a man hanging around a lamppost completely drunk. The conductor went to the driver and said, 'Look at him.' The bus driver looked and said, 'Oh my, what a pity it is not me. Never mind, it is my turn next week.' I knew that Scotland had quite a reputation for drink and much later, when treating patients and alcoholics, I realised just how big that problem actually is in Scotland.

CHAPTER FIVE

Nunspeet – A Profitable Village

There are many people who think that I have made a lot of money in Scotland and in alternative medicine. That is not really true, but I do admit that we made a lot of money in pharmacy in a small village called Nunspeet. Let me tell the story.

On 2 January 1960, I went by train from my birthplace of Kampen to Nunspeet. I had a special mission as I was to meet Dr Vogel, the man I had met in 1959 and with whom I had since been in contact in Holland. Dr Vogel had just bought a house called Roode Wald; a lovely old mansion with a lot of wooded grounds. With the help of others, his ambition was to set up the first nature cure clinic in Holland. That day, he asked me if I could help as it was essential that he employed someone who was qualified to dispense medicines and also he wanted us to work together to make his clinic successful. It had all the necessary requisites to become an absolutely wonderful clinic, so I decided to accept his offer and, with the help of others, turn this building into a magnificent place.

Roode Wald became a marvellous clinic. In the early stages when we were trying to build up the business, the general

manager, a charming gentleman (who was also friendly with Dr Vogel), and his wife dealt with the day-to-day running of the business, while I concentrated on dealing with the treatments and medicines. I foresaw lots of difficulties though – the nurses were not always the easiest people to deal with, and there were also some very dishonest staff ranging from housekeepers to domestic staff, so we had great problems. The positive side of all this was the focus on the remedies made by Dr Vogel, and on some of the remedies we made together. They started to become well known in Holland and, in turn, the business started to flourish. However, I realised that the management of the clinic could not continue as it was although, despite the many difficulties we had (which mainly centred around the staff), the care and attention given to the patients was not affected and their health was helped greatly.

One night, the head nurse called me to come over as something disastrous had happened. The general manager was at a conference in Germany and, that night, his wife had run away with many of their possessions. He was so devastated when he returned that he felt like giving up. With no government help or grants, it was very difficult to keep the business operating. I therefore decided to ask Dr Vogel to come over one Sunday to speak to all the staff, and he asked them all if they were fully behind him and if they were men of their word – was it yes yes, or no no? I can still hear him saying this.

A lot of the staff we employed were not as caring or devoted to people's health as they could have been. The staff problems – drunken nurses, theft and unreliable doctors – created a difficult situation. Dutch law stipulated that a medically qualified doctor had to be in charge of the therapies. However, we soon realised that medical doctors specialising in alternative

medicine were very scarce in those days, and we therefore had no alternative but to employ some unsavoury characters sometimes. I remember one who had long hair, tied back with a pink ribbon. Eventually it got so dirty that it was almost black and we realised that he could not be allowed to treat patients. Then we employed another doctor who developed a phobia of sunshine and would always walk around wearing dark glasses. I remember he once visited my wife on a wintry, snowy day wearing sandals without socks, and asked her if he could sit on the terrace outside to have his cup of tea. We employed some very eccentric characters; but although these doctors didn't really do any work, we had to take them on in order to satisfy the authorities. My book *Who's Next?*, which I wrote some time ago, is full of very funny stories about characters like these and also about patients I have treated over the years. Some of these stories are really unbelievable.

Being Dr Vogel's friend, I advised him that it would be better if he sold the business as, the way things were at that time, there was no future for Roode Wald. On the other hand, I felt it would be a good idea to continue producing the remedies so that the Dutch people could still benefit from them. So, after running the business for three years, we finally reached the decision to close the clinic but continue to manufacture the remedies.

After leaving Roode Wald, the first thing we did was to set up a sales office in Nunspeet and then one in The Hague. I was appointed director of the whole operation and things improved greatly from then on. Bioforce – or Biohorma in Dutch – became very well known. We then concentrated on building up the little business we had in The Hague, which was being managed by Mr Bolle. I shall never forget when Mr Bolle, Mr Drenth (one of the directors of Bioforce in Holland)

and myself met in Utrecht and, on the stairs of Hotel Terminus, made a decision to establish a factory at Elburg in Holland. We initially set up business in the house next to where Mr Bolle lived and later gradually started to build up the company in Elburg which, with a workforce of nearly 500 and a large turnover, became one of the biggest and most successful businesses in Holland. That was something to be really proud of.

That was not the only wonderful thing that happened in Nunspeet. As the village was such a lovely place to holiday in and had a beautiful hotel called Hotel Ittmann, I thought it would also make a charming place to get married. My future wife and I were very lucky because I had heard about a piece of land (roughly two acres) which I could buy extremely reasonably. We built our first house there and called it 'Tukien'.

It was a glorious summer's day when we got married in Nunspeet and, as I had already made a name for myself, it was a very big wedding, where the police had to direct the traffic outside the hotel because a lot of well-wishers had come along. We treasured the little house we had built, and three of our children were born there. It was a marvellous way for us to start married life. Everything went well, there in the woods of Holland with its beautiful scenery, not far from the secret village I wrote about in *Do Miracles Exist?* We were both very busy and, although I was building up Dr Vogel's business, something else happened that brought us a lot of money. The biggest pharmacy in the province was located in this village. It was well known throughout Holland for the many different items it sold. The owners were delightful people and Mr Hiddink, its owner, who was also a famous artist, had an interesting circle of friends. They were all local artists and we

soon became friendly with this wonderful bunch of people. Although perhaps not famous in Holland at that time, they certainly became famous later as artists – people like Jos Lussenburg, Chris ten Bruggenkate, Briett and others. Mr and Mrs Hiddink had a daughter called Herma. She became like a sister to me as we worked together sometimes. Mr Hiddink wanted to devote more of his time to painting and, as he knew I was a pharmacist, asked if I would be interested in taking over their business. It was a difficult decision as we had just got married and had little money but, after a lot of consideration, we decided to take the plunge. After we took over the business we had lots of fun running it, and I rebuilt it three times during our ownership. It expanded into five businesses under one roof, employing a staff of almost 30 people. Not only was it a pharmacy, but it was also the biggest photographic business in the district and the first place in Holland where films were developed and photographs ready within a few hours. It became well known and the turnover was astonishing. In all fairness, we made a lot of money there.

In the '60s, we opened another two pharmacy businesses and Joyce, my wife, took control of the photography side. She cleverly completed a four-year course in photography in just one year and became very well known in this field.

Running these businesses was very time-consuming but, on top of that, I still found time to work with Dr Vogel building up Bioforce. However, business was not really my scene: I have always said that I am not a businessman. My heart was with people and my aim in life was to help others. Although I worked hard to help people in the course of my work in the pharmaceutical business, I felt I wanted to do more, so I started lecturing on health, and these talks were very well attended. In between, I managed to visit countries throughout

the world with Dr Vogel where we studied the way in which people from other countries lived, what they did and why certain illnesses were unheard of in certain parts of the world. I had already studied the Vogel philosophies and the way in which he produced the medicines. We had even been to Switzerland several times to study the manufacturing process of medicines. I advised Dr Vogel that this was the only way in which we could make his business profitable. I was therefore the first person to set up a manufacturing plant in Holland. We started on a small scale, but the plant soon grew and is now so big that it also makes herbal remedies for other companies and is a great success.

I wanted to study more and go to China, and so I came out of the Dutch operation altogether in 1962 with enough money to enable me to further my studies. I wanted to know all about osteopathy (which I studied in Germany and then later in Holland). At the end of 1959, I had treated a Roman Catholic priest with very severe neck pain. During the course of our conversation, he mentioned that he sometimes worked in China and told me all about the philosophies of acupuncture. This whetted my appetite so much that I had a strong desire to go to China and learn about it. The priest said that this would be very difficult to do, but that through the Red Cross it could probably be arranged for me to go to a place where acupuncture was studied. I waived his fee of course, and much later, thinking about this conversation, I wrote to him. Lo and behold, he managed to get me into China, for which I shall always be very grateful. Anyone who wants to know about acupuncture needs to understand the philosophies behind it. I had first-class masters to help me with this, especially Professor Tsjang, who was of great assistance during my career and was the first man in the world who could show the

existence of meridians. I gathered quite a lot of knowledge on this subject during my time there. I also worked with Dr Jan Wei Tan in Kowloon, Hong Kong. Dr Tan adapted acupuncture so that it could be used to treat Westerners.

However, I think I gained most knowledge while working in the Veterans' Hospital in Taipei, Taiwan. I had the most wonderful time there and, along with the other students, learned not only about classic acupuncture but also about homoeopuncture – the method of dipping needles into homoeopathic solutions and inserting them in the acupuncture points. Although we would never be permitted to practise acupuncture in this country as we did in the Veterans' Hospital, it was still great experience. I remember very clearly working with a doctor who gave me the opportunity of gaining some practical experience in this field. She said I could take the cases I wanted, plus some of the difficult ones, which I was very pleased about. At one point, I was most astonished when the doctor brought a patient with Bell's palsy before me. She asked me how I treated people with Bell's palsy in Britain, and when I told her a smile appeared on her face. She asked the patient to lie down and then took an enormous, long needle, inserted it at the side of the patient's cheek, behind the eye, right to the brain, twiddled the needle a bit and then pulled it out. The Bell's palsy had disappeared! I nearly fainted in disbelief at what I had just witnessed and asked the doctor what would have happened if this woman had developed a haematoma. She said in China that is the patient's responsibility. Fortunately, in most other countries, the minute a patient walks through the doctor's door, the doctor is responsible for the well-being of that patient.

I saw quite a few amazing things and at the same time learned a lot. I felt very privileged that the Chinese disclosed

their secret knowledge of some very important acupuncture points to me as there is still a great deal of secrecy in China concerning the various acupuncture points they have discovered and worked with. That was a most interesting time in my life, and was to be of great assistance in my career.

❧ ❧ ❧

Here we are, back in Nunspeet in 1963. It is an absolutely wonderful place which brought us as a family a lot of prosperity. Nunspeet had so much to offer and I will always remember the many happy times we had there.

One particularly happy moment was when the village celebrated its freedom from the Nazis. Because of my British connections, the provost of the village asked if I could find out the name of the captain or commander in charge who finally freed Nunspeet from the Germans. This was a difficult job, but I finally traced this gentleman to Kent and asked him if he could come over to parade through the village in a Polar Bear Brigade jeep, giving the 'V' sign to show that we had been freed from the Germans. This he agreed to do. My friend, Jos Lussenburg, and I had a discussion and agreed to organise an enormous festival in the local Orange Park, where the flame of freedom that Captain Strawson was to ignite was positioned. Not long after we had organised this event, we managed to find out the original base of the Polar Bear Brigade. We had a great time re-enacting how Nunspeet was freed from the Nazis in 1945. Our local circle of friends all had a wonderful time and when Captain Strawson went through the village in the front of the jeep giving the 'V' sign, with Jos Lussenburg and me sitting in the back, we really had a lot of fun. Nunspeet certainly brought us a lot of happiness and, in

addition to this, as I have already said, we had a lot of good fortune in business, turning the local pharmacies into the biggest in the district.

Of course, building up Bioforce and the pharmacies took a lot of time. During the years that we worked and lived in Nunspeet, even although we were both very busy, we still managed to have all of our four children there. The first to be born was Fiona, in April 1961. My father and mother were still alive then and, as they also lived in the same village, they were of great help to us in looking after the children. Fiona qualified in nursing and went to work for the health service. Later on, she worked as a health visitor before securing an important post in London. She now has two children, both very gifted in music.

Our second daughter, Janyn, was born in April 1963 and, as we were convinced that she was going to be a boy, up until the moment she was born we didn't have a name for her. I remember going into Angelicq's house (our friend who lived across the road) and my wife, Joyce, and I looked at each other when she asked me what we were going to call the new baby. I replied 'Janyn' and Joyce said, 'Funnily enough, that was the name I had in mind.' Janyn studied science and is now married to Dr Tan. They both later took over and became managing directors of Bioforce UK, after Dr Tan had helped me to run my practices in Scotland. Janyn and Jen have three very intelligent children.

Our third daughter, Tertia ('the third'), was born in February 1967 and married a Dutchman. She studied as a medical herbalist and manages one of our clinics. Tertia and her husband, Michiel, are also very happily married and have two lovely children. Michiel worked in the same place as I did when I was later in Holland.

By the time Mhairi, our youngest daughter, was born in August 1969, we had moved to a new home which was called 'de Berken'. She studied osteopathy and married one of her lecturers in that subject. They now have a big practice in London and three wonderful boys.

So, Nunspeet was not only prosperous financially, but was also prosperous in that it gave us four wonderful daughters of whom, along with their families, we are very proud.

As life went on, we began to feel that we wanted to spend a bit more time with our daughters. We considered taking a sabbatical and going over to Scotland to my wife's family home, to spend at least a year with the children. We decided to keep our house in Holland and possibly return to live there after our sabbatical had come to an end. However, when we arrived in Scotland in 1970, I fell totally in love with the country. We bought a huge property in Troon which we decided to call Mokoia. It had about 40 rooms and, because it was so big, we felt that the most practical thing to do was to convert it into flats. However, when Dr Vogel came over and set eyes on Mokoia, he had different ideas. He said, 'This is a wonderful place – why don't we set up a residential clinic here? It would be a great opportunity for people who live in this part of the world to be given the chance of being introduced to nature cures.' I looked at the magnificent property and realised he was right. Why should we keep such beauty to ourselves? Why not get the whole place sorted out and open it as a clinic? Over the years, I had studied widely in alternative treatments and was particularly interested in such areas as homoeopathy, osteopathy, acupuncture and naturopathy. I had also undertaken several studies on these subjects. I felt I had to think about Dr Vogel's suggestion seriously.

This was emphasised when God sent a little angel to see me one very rainy Sunday afternoon. A lady stood at the front door and asked my name. She said that we had studied certain forms of homoeopathy and breathing exercises under the same professor in Germany. That was Professor von Durckheim. We had a wonderful conversation and realised we had a lot in common. Many Scottish people will still know this lady – Dr Annelie Hennessy. Not only was she very well respected in Glasgow, but she was also a consultant at the Homoeopathic Hospital. Dr Hennessy thought that Mokoia would make a wonderful place in which to treat patients and that I should start a residential clinic there as soon as possible. I grew even more determined to do so. We thought long and hard about it and decided to get the property completely in order. As it transpired, the chosen name for the house was very apt, as Mokoia means 'Island of Rest'.

We made up our minds to set up this new clinic in Troon and to say goodbye to good old Nunspeet. This was very difficult because we had to leave all our friends and family there, but I really felt that setting up this clinic in Scotland was my calling. I loved the people, I loved the country and, once more, that old biblical saying 'It is not in man that walketh to direct his steps' (Jeremiah 10:23) came to mind. The decision was made to take the first step into a completely new and unknown venture. We had to start from scratch, but the business soon started to grow and continued to expand on an unbelievable scale.

But now, I would like to say a little more on my children and grandchildren.

Four-Leaf Clover

We have been richly blessed with four beautiful daughters, each with her own charm. At each birth, I wondered if this time it would be a boy. However, they were all girls and this was probably lucky; they have all given us such a lot of pleasure and, as daughters are usually very devoted to their fathers, I am very fortunate. They are a nice mixture of nationalities, with Dutch, German, Jewish, English, Scottish and Irish blood. I suppose the combination of genes was helpful as they all did well at school and, thankfully, were never any trouble to Joyce or myself.

Because my wife had worked in education and knew more about child psychology than I did, I told her she could take the lead and that she could rely on my total support in their upbringing. They were a real pleasure as they were growing up. As they are now all married, our lives have been further enriched by the addition of ten grandchildren – all with a wonderful mixture of Dutch, Scottish, English, Irish, German, Jewish, Chinese and Singaporian blood.

I treasure every one of my daughters and each has such great qualities. They all played their part in helping me in the

clinic as they were growing up and I encouraged them all to do a stint at the reception desk when I was practising. This brought them into contact with people and, during their school holidays, they were very helpful in assisting me whenever necessary. This sometimes did not always meet with the greatest enthusiasm because they felt their father was strict and Victorian, but that was the way I was brought up and I tried to instil in them that life was not easy and could sometimes be quite difficult.

Sometimes it was with great hilarity that they undertook their work and I well remember the time when my eldest daughter, Fiona – who was still at school when she helped with reception work – once knocked on my door and, with a long face, showed in a very nice female patient whom she thought was after her father. She opened the door for this lady and said, 'Daaaad, this is your next patient, but Mum needs you.' This was to make absolutely certain that the well-dressed and made-up lady knew I was married. I later asked Fiona why she had said that and she told me that she had become suspicious because the lady in question had been in the cloakroom for about half an hour putting on her make-up and dolling herself up. This was just one of the funny things that happened when my daughters attended to patients at the reception desk.

When she grew up, I was so proud to see Fiona succeeding in her nursing career and later on, with her nursing degree, she obtained a very responsible job in London. I was happy that she too wanted to help others. She married Peter, a very good artist who came from Dorset and set up a successful business in Troon – a framework gallery that not only showcases his own work but also that of other artists. He handles some of the most beautiful paintings, which is lucky for me as I have a weakness for paintings. They are blessed

with two wonderful children. The oldest one, Michael, has an exceptional aptitude for music and plays the violin and piano. The genes of both my family and his father's family are evident in him. As there were so many well-known musicians in my family, Michael has inherited a talent going back generations on both my mother's and father's side. I can never overestimate how proud I am when I see him performing in big halls full of people and the applause that he gets for his talents. His younger sister, Rachel, very clever at school, also has a gift for music.

My second daughter, Janyn, to whom I have been very close since the day she was born, developed a strong flair for business that became evident from an early age. She had a little friend called Freddy. One day, they disappeared together and we could not find them anywhere. We were almost frantic with worry until they eventually returned with a bag full of coins. Janyn had suggested to her little friend that they look for acorns, gather them in big bags and sell them to the farmers, demonstrating a business aptitude when they were still at nursery and very young! It is therefore not surprising that she graduated with a degree in science and business studies and is now the managing director of Bioforce, the British arm of Biohorma, the company set up by Dr Vogel and I. When I told the story to Dr Vogel, he thought it was amazing that she had such flair. I thought it would be an excellent idea to put these business skills to good use in forming what was to become a leading company in herbal and homoeopathic medicine. Janyn married a very clever young doctor, who had great prospects in medicine but, luckily, they were both so business-minded that he joined her and together they have built up a very big business which is not only of great assistance to the well-being of many people, but also to the entire industry, as the research

they undertake with their company benefits the field of alternative medicine and also provides employment for many people.

My first grandchild, Li-Anna, was a product of these two. Li-Anna was a most wonderful baby and when she was born it sank in that I was now a grandfather for the first time. I did not like the thought of that at all! Having a Peter Pan complex of always wanting to feel young, I had to get used to the idea. I have often heard parents saying what a marvellous feeling it is when they become grandparents. I never really understood that fully until Li-Anna was born, when I enjoyed the gift of my first grandchild. I have found having grandchildren to be one of the most wonderful experiences in my life. As Li-Anna was growing up and starting to talk, it was suggested that she called us Grandma and Granddad, but my wife and I did not want this at all. My daughter then said to me, 'You must not be so grumpy' and, from that moment, we were called 'Mumpy' and 'Grumpy'. As Li-Anna couldn't say the word 'Grumpy', she called me 'Dumpy' instead and, to this day, every grandchild I have calls me 'Dumpy'. She was always very caring and I experienced that only a few Saturdays ago, while in the process of writing this autobiography. Her parents were abroad on business and their nanny was looking after all three of the children at home. On this particular Saturday afternoon, when I was busy attending to many patients at Auchenkyle, I suddenly saw Li-Anna floating around outside my consulting room window. When she caught my eye, she came to the window and said, 'Dumpy, I came to see if you were all right.' As a grandparent, it tugs at your heartstrings when a young girl of 14 cares so much for her grandfather that she has to come and make sure he is all right. It is a feeling that is difficult to put into words but, nevertheless, so heart-

warming to experience. Joni, her little brother, who is named after me, has a great technical brain. He loves playing with his train set and planes, just as I used to do as a boy. The youngest one, Harriet, is a most humorous child who always amazes me with the way she chooses her words. Looking at this happy family, I am grateful for these great gifts.

My third daughter, Tertia, resembles me in looks the most and is also identical in character. She was in the limelight shortly after she was born when she appeared in the local newspapers as the best-looking baby in the town and was pictured being held by Miss Holland. As a baby she was photographed many times. She has a tremendous sense of humour and a gift for cheering people up when they are depressed or down and, because she works with me and manages the clinic in Ayr, she is greatly loved by the patients there. When I went to Holland to undertake my research work, Tertia came with me to assist with the project to test allergies, as she was a qualified medical herbalist. She was of great help in the clinical and research work we set up in Holland. There was a wonderful boy, Michiel, who worked at that clinic during his holidays, a very serious fellow who worked with great devotion. He became attracted to Tertia, with her usual charm, and it was a surprise to me when she told me that they both wanted to talk to my wife and myself about their friendship. They got on very well together and, after a while, became engaged and, later on, got married. They then announced that they were going to Canada where Michiel, a real Dutchman, had a business in snowmobiles. They went to Bathurst where they started their business and were there for a number of years before returning to Holland. Thankfully, they now live quite near us. Their first baby was called Gemma. She stole our hearts and I have written about her in

many of my books. She was a little miracle, as she weighed only 1lb 8oz when she was born. However, she has grown up to be the most loving girl and is now doing very well. Some time later, her little brother, Dale, was born. He is the image of his mother and, therefore, of myself. It is amazing how you can see yourself in your children and grandchildren, and he is exactly like us in many ways. Although he is only a year old, I can still see some of my mannerisms in him. They very much enjoy family life and it is a great delight to see the children playing together. Dale has a mischievous nature similar to his mother's as she was growing up. I remember when we were staying in the Grand Hotel in Toronto that Tertia, at about the age of five, sneakily turned around all the 'Do Not Disturb' signs on the bedroom doors so that they read 'Please Make Up The Room'. The chambermaids wakened up all the confused guests, who managed to see the funny side when they realised what Tertia had done. On another occasion, when we went to the Deer Park at Loch Lomond, she turned round all the signs to point in the opposite direction and that caused great chaos. These were some of the little sneaky things she did that made everyone laugh.

My fourth daughter, Mhairi, was also born in Nunspeet. She was the least good-looking when she was born. My friend, the doctor who was there at the birth, said that she would be very beautiful one day, and he was right. She is now the best-looking girl of the four, and the older she gets the more beautiful she becomes. Every time I see her, I can hardly believe she is my daughter. She has a very serious character and was therefore very precise at school, very correct in her speaking and writing. Nowadays, she often writes for magazines and newspapers. She, of course, came from Holland to Scotland and it was quite funny when she mixed English

ABOVE: Kampen, the little
place where I was born.

BELOW: At kindergarten – the
building was not unlike Auchenkyle.

RIGHT: One of the clinics in Holland.

BELOW: Biohorma, Holland. I was one of the founders.

ABOVE: Dr Vogel – still teaching me!

BELOW: Auchenkyle, still in full use as a clinic.

The clinic interior in
Ayr.

In conversation with HRH
the Duchess of Gloucester.

ABOVE: The whole family.

BELOW: In the Australian bush.

ABOVE: Preaching
the message of health
in Edinburgh.

RIGHT: With Gloria
Hunniford.

ABOVE: In Portland, Oregon, with two children who had been conceived due to the help of natural medicine.

BELOW: In one of the world tours at the Botanical Gardens in Melbourne, Australia.

ABOVE: In Chicago, USA, for consultations.

RIGHT: In one of my meetings with Prince Charles.

nouns with Dutch grammar and verbs. Her teacher would often laugh, telling her colleagues that Mhairi had said, 'That's how you *don't* do it.' She went on to study osteopathy and her lecturer, a very lovely young man, recognised her beauty. When we were told that her lecturer had fallen in love with her and they both wanted to tell us how happy they were, they hoped we would give them our approval. Marcus, now her husband, is a great friend to me. We do a lot of things together and, as he has his own clinic, I often help him and vice versa. On the many times that we travel to and from the airport, we have the most interesting discussions and the most profitable business meetings, where we talk about our ideas, the formulation of remedies and compare these with patients' results. Mhairi and Marcus produced three good-looking boys, all very sporty. One of them, Jonathan, who is now aged six, is already very advanced at playing tennis. Cameron, serious like his mother, is very thoughtful. It was an emotional moment when he thought I was very worried about something. He came up to me and put his arm around me and said, 'Dumpy, I love you.' The youngest, Oliver, is a bit like myself – always on the go, in perpetual motion and full of mischief. The three of them once appeared on television with me on *This Morning* with Richard and Judy. They behaved unbelievably well when they were asked lots of questions.

It is amazing to see how my grandchildren have developed. Although all ten have different qualities and characteristics, there are similarities between them.

❧ ❧ ❧

My daughters were all born in Holland and could only speak Dutch when they came to Britain. My wife and I were often criticised for not hiring the services of an English tutor. We

actually did this on purpose. Being in the teaching profession, my wife had often seen how quickly children pick up a new language in the classroom, and learn much quicker that way, so we decided to let our daughters learn like that rather than putting the extra burden on them of having a tutor teach them a foreign language. The wisdom of that decision was evident when they obtained very high grades in their English Highers.

So, we have been very fortunate with our children and grandchildren, who are all so happy and healthy. When I cast my mind back to the days when my children were small and I took them out with their bicycles or for little walks, I often regret that I was not able to spend more time with them. My work has taken up such a lot of my time that perhaps my family life was sacrificed a little. In retrospect, I now feel I should have given more time to my children. As one gets older, there is nothing more regrettable than not having made more of life and enjoying family life to the full when one's children are small. To have healthy children is a great gift. Now my daughters have all established themselves so well, and life has so much to offer them.

CHAPTER SEVEN

Mokoia – 'Island of Rest'

Mokoia was a beautiful mansion overlooking the Clyde, with the most marvellous features and a library like I have never seen before, built from the roots of a walnut tree. There is a love story about the island of Mokoia in New Zealand, where Hinamoa, a Maori prince, finds his princess on the island of Rotorua. It is such a beautiful story and very touching. The spirit of the house was very invigorating and the atmosphere of the whole place was like a breath of fresh air.

However, to bring the house up to the standard required to transform it into a clinic, a great deal of work had to be done. A lot of refurbishment took place and we worked for a whole year to get the property in order. After all the work had been completed, we thought it would make a wonderful clinic. It was therefore a great shock to me when – after all the work had been completed, with everything looking absolutely beautiful, and we were ready for business – there was no interest in it at all. Many days I prayed very hard for God to send patients because I was itching to get started, after the busy times that I previously had in Holland, where I led a very full life.

The children had all gone to school – some to nursery,

others to primary school – and my wife felt that as all our money had gone into renovating the property, she had to go back to teaching in order to help financially, and so she took up a job as a teacher.

Gradually, the Scottish people became curious about what we had to offer and soon people started to stream in. As well as the residential clinic, we also had a day clinic. The residential clinic soon became full and the day clinic also started to get busier and busier. I managed to find some great staff to help me, especially my physiotherapist, Janice Thompson, and later Teresa Sampson. We also arranged seminars and it gives me a lot of pleasure to think back to the great days when we gave yoga and teaching seminars. A few of our successes became known and many people then wanted to be helped. The osteopathic and acupuncture clinics grew very quickly and we soon had our hands full.

In those early days, I remember one of the female patients we had who was quite ill and had been confined to her bed for years. After treatment, she was like a new person and was able to return home. A lot of other patients then followed, as this was seen as a miracle. A young Rangers footballer who had given up playing also came to me for help. After he had completed his treatment at the clinic, the papers were full of stories of how this young man had regained his health. Another lady, who came from the Isle of Arran and had to be brought in on a stretcher, returned home after three weeks of receiving treatment and was able to walk again. After that miracle, nearly half of Arran became patients!

Things were going very well and, as we needed healthy food for the kitchen at the clinic, I went to the local health food store. They never usually stocked the items we needed, so I tried to get the addresses of their suppliers from the lady who

owned the shop. She asked if I would be interested in taking over her business, and that was how I bought my first health food store. I had planned to close it but, one evening after I had taken over, the lady who worked there came to my door and asked if I would keep it going as she loved working there and would do her best to run the shop, so I would have no problems. I decided to give it a try. I helped her a little bit and, after we started work on it, the store grew. It enabled us to provide the right products at the right time.

Strangely, similar problems arose at the residential clinic as had come up in Holland. We had many problems finding domestic staff to do the cleaning and staff to look after the patients. This made things very difficult and, for almost the same reasons as Dr Vogel and I had to close the Dutch clinic, we decided to close the residential clinic in Scotland. I found this a very difficult decision. However, I still wanted to be able to help patients, so we reopened as a day clinic only, which was a great success and very busy. We opened this six days a week from 7 a.m. to 10 p.m. Patients came from all over the world and, as these included a lot of famous people, the clinic soon developed a reputation and we were sometimes so busy that I could hardly cope.

We already used some of Dr Vogel's remedies that I had brought from Holland, but we wanted to be able to stock the whole range of his products. As Dr Vogel had an importer in England, Joe Bennett, from Chorley in Lancashire, I contacted him to see if he could provide the extra medicines I needed to treat all my patients. We met on a Monday morning at Carlisle station, together with his friend, Bert Barlow. We discussed different options and Joe finally offered me the whole range of Dr Vogel's imported remedies if I was willing to take a clinic once a month in his premises in Chorley. I naturally accepted

his offer and still honour it now, 30 years later, by taking clinics there on the second Monday of each month.

I have many memories of these monthly visits as, when I started there in 1970, a lot of time was spent travelling to and from the clinics. I used to leave on the night train on Sunday about 11 o'clock and arrive in Carlisle at around 1 o'clock in the morning. On my arrival at Carlisle station in the middle of the night, I sometimes had to spend three-quarters of an hour – or sometimes even a full hour – waiting for a connection to Preston. Because of these long waits, I sometimes witnessed such disturbing scenes – fights and other unspeakable things – in the waiting-room that I had to leave. On one particular night I was nearly attacked by a drunken youth and had to leave very quickly.

When I arrived at Preston the first time, Joe Bennett was there to meet me. Having had just a few hours' sleep, I started the clinic at 7 a.m. for 7.30 a.m. When I arrived at the clinic, the place was usually as packed as Lourdes. My practice was open all day, plus the evening, and then I had to leave in the middle of the night to go back to Troon and see patients that morning. This was a very hectic time, but travel has improved greatly since then and I still attend the clinic so as not to disappoint patients.

Mokoia was growing bigger and, after Joe had given us the import of the Bioforce products, we formed a company called Swiss Health Products. We initially promoted the business by advertising the wonderful remedies that Dr Vogel made and, with a lot of work, we built up this company, until my second daughter, Janyn, who by now had a degree in business science, started Bioforce UK in the 1980s.

Mokoia was a busy place and it was with great regret that, because of overheads, we had to sell. As it was such a big place,

a local builder who had inspected the property felt that it could be converted into flats. At the time we opened Mokoia as a residential clinic, we had also bought a house in Ottoline Drive in Troon and moved our family there. The property was quite small, and our lawyer mentioned that he had heard there was a house situated in part of an estate called Auchenkyle which was for sale. On a lovely Sunday morning, we went to have a look at this property and, indeed, South Auchenkyle was for sale. My mother was visiting us at that time. She had a strong sense of intuition, and felt that we should buy this property. I too felt that it would be a very good choice. Many times in life I have followed my intuition, and it has never failed me.

There are five tangible senses – vision, hearing, taste, smell and touch. However, there is also a sense which often is said to be a 'clairvoyant' sense. I disagree with this, as I believe it is actually intuition. There is a theory that this sense has a lot to do with breathing and, as I have always said, the way we breathe is a very important part of life and has a tremendous effect on life in general. The sense of intuition has been, for me, of great importance throughout my life and, not only has it been of great help to me when treating patients, but in other areas too, and it has never let me down. The decision to purchase South Auchenkyle was the right one to make and I will go into this in more detail in Chapter Nine.

During the latter part of the time we lived in Mokoia, Dr Vogel depended on me and I had to go to Switzerland several times to help him with business matters and also to advise him on many of the Bioforce affairs. Although I thought I knew this little man very well already, I got to know him much better during that period and also started to lecture throughout the world with him. I learned more about his philosophies and his lifestyle during my travels with him.

CHAPTER EIGHT

Dr Alfred Vogel – A Genius

D r Alfred Vogel was a remarkable little man. Wherever he went, he always had an audience. I have spoken about him earlier in this autobiography, but Vogel played a great role in my life. He often said that we clicked at that very first meeting, and I totally agree with him. Usually at his big lectures, he would talk to me and ask me what I thought about certain things, as he knew he had found a true follower in me. I was the only person in the world that he really taught. Because he was so busy attending to people's health, he never had enough time to devote to teaching, which was a great pity, although he imparted a lot of his knowledge to others through his books and lectures, and was never afraid to share his thoughts about life in general. There were generations of wise people in his family, who come from a little place called Asch, right across from the Ida Wegmann Institute, the Anthroposophical Institute of Rudolph Steiner, where Dr Vogel was born. This little place holds lots of memories of Vogel. There is a museum in honour of him, to which he gifted many artefacts that he collected from other countries during his travels. He learned a lot from his grandmother, a

great lady who knew a tremendous amount about herbs. His whole heart and soul was devoted to nature cure. From a young age, it was all he was interested in. His enormous knowledge and thirst for what nature had to offer took him to many underdeveloped countries in the world, where he loved to study methods used by other nationalities. He also tried to discover why certain illnesses were unheard of in certain countries. He gained a tremendous amount of information from his family while he was growing up, and then began to treat people himself.

He bought a little house right on the hill overlooking Teufen near St Gallen. During his travels throughout the world he gathered a lot of knowledge and I still remember busloads of people coming to his first little clinic. Like myself, he started with a small residential clinic, but later became so busy with patients that he had to close the residential side. He also wanted to produce his own medicines for his patients and to manufacture these to the very highest quality. He and his wife Sophie, whom I also greatly respected, did as much as they could to help others.

I would like to say a little about my first visit to Teufen, and later my last visit to Dr Vogel's beautiful home, completely organically built, in Feusiberg. As I have said earlier, I met Dr Vogel in Holland and worked with him at his first clinic of nature cure in Holland. I told him that, in order for his business to survive, we had to manufacture as many products as possible locally in order to reduce costs and allow the products to be easily accessible to patients. He agreed, and the time then came for us to go to Switzerland to learn about the procedures involved. I was newly married at that time and my wife decided to come with me. We arrived in Teufen, where other doctors were taking his clinics, as Vogel was

completely involved in his organic garden, covering a field with manure himself, which was something he loved doing. He was not at all pleased by our arrival, as we were disturbing him and he wanted to get on with the garden. He really didn't make us feel very welcome and we were quite upset when his manager took us to a little hotel called Schafiliegg. As the Swiss people were very small, our heads could touch the ceiling of our room!

The next day, we went to start work and luckily Vogel was a little friendlier this time. However, before we started, we went to a lawyer and I became the only person in the world to have control over all the recipes and their manufacture. This was all signed and sealed and then we started work. It was very hard. Dr Vogel taught us along with his doctor, Dr Reinmalt, and his fantastic manager, Herr Metler. We put a lot of energy into learning the processes and we not only had to write everything down, but we also had meetings and training sessions. Finally, because I was a pharmacist, I took the whole operation in hand, and went back to Holland to commence the manufacturing process, which is still done at Bioforce today.

Dr Vogel and I became friends and trusted each other. We talked a lot and, as his ideas on business and religion were quite extreme, we had some heated discussions. This little man had a very sober lifestyle, kept strictly to a healthy diet and was very fit. He was usually in bed by nine o'clock in the evening, but then he would be in the clinic by four or five o'clock the next morning to deal with his massive correspondence. His staff found working for him very difficult. They all had to work extremely hard, which resulted in the highest standard of quality control I have ever seen. If anything was not up to standard, it had to be thrown away. He

built up the business very well and gave it his full attention.

It was wonderful to listen to Vogel's poetry and wise sayings. A lot of these sayings were very dear to me and one which I remember was, 'In nature, everything is in harmony. Everything remains in harmony if man does not interfere.' He also had wonderful sayings about creation. Wherever he went, he was bursting with enthusiasm, telling people how to preserve their health.

We became very close, especially when we went up into the mountains to discover more plants and flowers. He taught me about the characteristics and signatures of plants, herbs, roots and leaves. Many times when we were in the mountains, he would say, 'Here is arnica. If you stand on it, it will talk back to you. This is a sign from God that it should be used to treat trauma – that is the reason it makes a noise when you step on it.' Even after all these years, I still prescribe arnica for trauma. I was very pleased when Her Majesty the Queen once told me personally that her grandfather used to carry arnica in his pocket, and would give it to people if he saw little accidents happening.

Dr Vogel would fall to his knees and dig in the heavy lime clay in the Swiss Alps whenever he smelled wild garlic. He used to say to me, when it was very dirty and wet, 'Come and look at the garlic. Can you see that nothing of the earth will influence it? It is silvery white to show you that it is a great cleanser.' He also used to show me hypericum (St John's wort). Its leaves had little holes, filled with the wonderful St John's wort oil. This plant had the message: 'I am the plant of love. When you are depressed or even suicidal, take me with my loving signature, I want to heal you.' It was a wonderful experience. Later on, we went to other countries where he studied different plants, and every time when he returned after

discovering new plants and flowers, he considered what ailment they could be used to treat.

Our best teachers, though, were the gypsies. They taught us more about herbs during the time we spent with them in the mountains than the best professors of pharmacology. They were masters not only in finding herbs, but also knew so much about them and shared their knowledge with us. Often, when we could not find them, Vogel knew where they would be and went to the local pub for them. Drink was their greatest friend and the minute Dr Vogel had paid them, they would go off to the pub. They very seldom ate anything and when they were not with us in the mountains, they would drink gallons of Schuitzengarten beer. If we ever needed to find certain herbs and could not find the gypsies, one of the pubs could often tell us where they were, as they usually owed a lot of money. It was a wonderful time and we often stayed overnight in the mountains on warm summer evenings. For me, it was a great education.

❦ ❦ ❦

Back in Holland, I remember that when Janyn, my second daughter, was born, Dr Vogel held her in his arms and said, 'I wish you were a son so that you could become my successor. Now you will have to do it.' Little did he know then that Janyn would later become one of his best general managers.

In Holland, we had a lot of battles to fight building up Biohorma. I remember one day, after working very hard, Arie Drenth (a colleague of mine) and I went for something to eat. Vogel would usually only have a pear or an apple during the day, and would never think of taking time off to eat anything. He was almost completely addicted to helping people by

creating more and more remedies. He could not bear it if anything was wasted and I remember once, when I was making Santasapina cough mixture from pine nuts and pine needles, that he looked over and said, 'You cannot throw the residue away. We can make some good bath salts out of this.' This is a marvellous example of his thrifty character.

We both worked very hard in Holland, giving lectures to big gatherings in health food stores in order to keep the message alive, and also working on *The Nature Doctor* and its translation, which sold over 2.5 million copies in Holland alone – hard work but, nevertheless, very rewarding. When we started working together in Great Britain, he had the same enthusiasm and when we met various people at universities, everybody was astonished by his knowledge. He was absolutely delighted when we started Bioforce UK in Cramlington in Newcastle, so that his remedies and his books could be accessible to people throughout the country. People hung on every word and many loved him.

I often think that his life story was very similar to that of the greatest Jewish king who ever lived, King David, as he was also greatly gifted. In many ways, he was eccentric and difficult to work with, as he was a very impatient person, but from experience I knew that he was a genius and had a very high IQ. I have often felt that his daughters – especially one who was mentally affected – were probably a result of this. Ruth, one of his daughters, was a great friend to me and later on I often tried to follow in Vogel's footsteps. We were very concerned about him when his first wife, Sophie, died. Vogel became very depressed about this great loss and it took a lot of gentle persuasion to encourage him to try and find another wife as he was not the type of man who liked being on his own. He was very much a social character, and also needed to

be nurtured. Luckily, one of his former secretaries arrived on the scene and when he told me he was going to get remarried, I was very happy. As well as being a genius, Dr Vogel was quite an eccentric man. I remember he once asked me to bring my daughter, Janyn, over to visit him because he wanted to discuss the future of Britain.

I came out of the company in 1968 for a lot of reasons, one being that I didn't feel comfortable at the thought of making money from promoting the products. I told Dr Vogel that I did not want to stay in a company from which I was benefiting financially, and I felt that it would be better to leave it completely to my daughter and her husband to operate.

⁂ ⁂ ⁂

On one visit to Switzerland to meet Dr Vogel, my daughter and I had just met at the airport in London when I discovered that I had forgotten my passport. To get into Switzerland without a passport is virtually impossible, but I decided to try because I did not have enough time to go back and collect it. I thought that I could speak to Dr Vogel at the airport over a railing. My daughter and I were very worried because we knew how strict the Swiss were about passports.

A meeting had been arranged at Dr Vogel's house in Riehen. At the end of the journey, we arrived at Zurich passport control. Of course, we had no chance of getting into Switzerland, but I knew that Vogel and his wife were on the other side of passport control to meet us and, when I was asked at the control point what I was going to do, I said that I would only be there for a day, that I would leave my luggage and everything else with him and that I had a meeting with Dr Vogel. He said, 'Ah, Dr Vogel from Teufen?' I confirmed

that it was. He asked, 'Is this the man who wrote *The Nature Doctor?*' to which I replied, 'Yes. He is outside passport control. I know he is there waiting for us.' He kindly sent someone to find Dr Vogel and his new wife and ask them to go to passport control, where Vogel confirmed that we had meetings arranged and promised that he would personally make sure I was brought back to the airport the same evening. Incredibly, Janyn and I were allowed through.

I wish you could have seen Dr Vogel's reaction. For at least 15 minutes, he was incredulous that I had managed to get into Switzerland so easily. He said to me, 'If people can get into this country as easily as that, then what is this country coming to?' I told him that he should be proud of himself; it was because he had such a good name in Switzerland that my daughter and I had been allowed through. That finally settled him down and we had a wonderful meeting.

I could fill a whole book about the experiences that Vogel and I had wherever we travelled throughout the world. His sense of humour often managed to get us out of a lot of difficult situations. I dearly loved him and, when he went, I lost a very great friend.

Our last meeting was totally different from the first one. In 1998, a few weeks before he died, I spent a whole day with him. He was already not very well and, when I arrived, he became quite emotional. A lot of happy memories came into our minds and I was surprised at how sharp his mind was. He could still talk about our various business affairs throughout the world, the problems relating to medical acts and legal procedures, so he was well up to date. By the afternoon, he got a little tired, but he picked up when we started to talk about past experiences, and we had some good laughs. By five o'clock, it was time for me to leave. Before I left, I took a letter

out of my pocket from the Royal Free Hospital in London. The letter related to a patient who had incurable cancer. Unfortunately, although this girl had been through all the medical processes, she had not improved. When I saw her I took her into my care, using a lot of Vogel's remedies and also his philosophies and, luckily, she steadily improved. At long last the tumour, which had nearly reached her brain, had shrunk to such an extent that she was told by the oncologist that she could live a normal life. The oncologist, however, wanted to know what she had done and, when she told him, he said that he would write to me. This was the letter I had just taken out of my pocket, in which he said that he was not only surprised but also had great admiration for the way she was treated. He had monitored this girl and the work that was carried out on her, and wanted to know more about the remedies used. He asked if I would go over to the hospital and do some lectures on this subject and also tell them exactly the methods I used to treat this unfortunate girl, who could now lead a normal life. I read this letter to Dr Vogel before I left and I could see he was very moved. He embraced me and the feelings of over 40 years working together were very strong as, for the last time in this life, I had to say goodbye to him.

❧ CHAPTER NINE ❧

Auchenkyle – 'Beneath the Kyles'

Auchenkyle is the most beautiful place, set in 20 acres of woodland, looking over Auchenkyle Bridge to the Clyde with the beautiful Isle of Arran in the background. It is a place where many people have regained their health and found happiness. The Fraser family, in building Auchenkyle, spared no expense in making it a most attractive property, surrounded by rhododendrons, some of which are unique. When we first went there we lived in South Auchenkyle, but another family lived in North Auchenkyle, who did not appreciate its beauty and had done a lot of damage to the property. Some of its most beautiful trees had been felled like matchsticks and we could see, as neighbours, how much the place was being neglected. With a lot of diplomatic persuasion, I asked the owners of North Auchenkyle if they would consider selling. Finally, we were successful and bought it at a reasonable price. However, difficulties then arose in trying to get them to leave the property. Eventually my lawyer, John Mason, and I managed to get them out, but the damage that had been caused was quite extensive and it was necessary for many repairs to be carried out.

We renovated the property to its original state and started
our clinic there after Mokoia had been sold. Patients could
then attend Auchenkyle as a day clinic. The business rocketed
and, from then to this day, I have had to work very hard from
early morning until late evening in order to meet patients'
demands. People come from all over the world to try and find
help – the famous, the rich and the poor. We have had some
wonderful successes, which I will write about in a later
chapter, but the demands on me were so great that,
regrettably, I had to curtail some of my other work.
Unfortunately, I had to give up the clinic in Birmingham,
which I really loved, but could no longer keep this going as
other clinics had developed and I had to divide my time
between them. Through my book writing, I then got involved
in a tremendous amount of radio work, and television stations
also urged me to take part in some of their programmes.

I started with Gloria Hunniford in 1982, who then broadcast
on Radio 2. The programmes became a tremendous success
and even more so after Gloria broke her arm during a tennis
match and I was instrumental in helping to mend it very
quickly. Gloria, who was initially quite sceptical about
alternative medicine, became more and more interested. From
1982 until 1992, we did programmes together every month for
Radio 2. They became so successful that, after one programme,
nearly 10,000 letters were received. The demand became
greater and greater.

While broadcasting these programmes, I usually stayed in
the George Hotel, which was situated across from Langham
Church. A funny thing happened when patients discovered
where I was staying – they actually followed me there! On
leaving the hotel early in the morning, on my way to the radio
station to prepare for the programme at two o'clock, I was

amazed to find the hotel restaurant packed full of patients. I managed to see people in a side room and gave them free advice. However, this unofficial clinic became so busy that the hotel manager came to me at one point and said, 'Listen, this place is beginning to look like a hospital, with wheelchairs and ill people – you take over the whole place when you are here. Although we love the extra business this brings us, there have been objections from some of the residents. Would you be interested in possibly taking two rooms upstairs, which we would be willing to give you for nothing, as a lot of your patients would then stay overnight here?'

Unfortunately, as some of my patients found using the lifts and stairs a problem, I had to look for alternative premises from which to consult and, in 1983, found a place at 10 Harley Street. This was a very prestigious building and although there were about 60 other doctors practising there at that time, I decided to consult there on two days a month. As my patients in the London area had increased so much, we needed at least two days there to meet their demands. Everybody was quite happy and, at No. 10, I saw a lot of famous people – from royalty and film stars to politicians as well as the general public. People came from all over the world and I met some very interesting people and had some wonderful results. I became very friendly with the owners, who asked me if I would join the governing body at 10 Harley Street to discuss its further development. It was most interesting to see orthodox and alternative medical practitioners working together, and it was controlled by ethics. I saw quite a few amazing things there. We had a great team and everything went absolutely fine.

As I was coming up the stairs one day, I remember meeting a lady whom I had treated years before and had not seen since.

When I recognised her, I asked her why she was singing and looked so happy. 'Because,' she said, 'I came to you on a stretcher to Auchenkyle, brought by a private plane, with a letter from my doctor stating that I had a month to live.' She added that, after all these years, she was here to visit me just for a check-up. She said that I had cured her. I told her that I have never cured anyone – God cures, I only treat.

We saw many patients there. I loved the place and practised there with the greatest pleasure but, unfortunately, problems arose. On the two days when I was there, the consulting room was so full of my patients that the other doctors' patients couldn't find a seat. It was very sad, but we could find no other solution than to look for alternative rooms, which we later found at 53 Upper Montague Street – just a few streets away from Harley Street. However, the Harley Street premises were very much in my heart, as I remembered the many people I had seen there and how happy we had been. More work then came my way because of the publicity in newspapers and magazines, radio and television, and so we had to extend further.

Bioforce UK, which had established itself in Cramlington and was run by my daughter Janyn, also began to grow. Bioforce had got so much bigger that they needed some help. A lot of patients in the Newcastle area had also enquired about seeing me. As I was needed there at that time, it was decided that I would consult at Cramlington one day a month. Again, patients came from far and wide, and we were very busy there – so busy, in fact, that we again had to look for bigger premises, as Bioforce needed my consulting room to expand

the business. I found rooms in a very busy general practice. This was the first time in my life that I had worked as a practitioner in a doctor's practice. The cooperation between the doctors and myself was absolutely brilliant and patients who consulted me there were delighted. It was quite a sacrifice, as I had to get up at 4.30 in the morning to go by car, with my assistant, Teresa, to Newcastle to start work there before 8 a.m. We did not finish until 7 p.m., after which I then had to fly to London to consult at my Harley Street clinic after a hard day's work. However, we enjoyed it. We worked well together and learned such a lot from each other.

However, all the travelling made things very hard and, although we consulted at this clinic for many years, we got so busy and the travelling became so much more difficult due to congestion that we finally decided to give it up after being stranded on the A74 one evening. I shall never forget that evening – I have never seen so much ice and snow and misery. We were sandwiched between large lorries on the road and it made us realise how dreadful travelling could really be. So, after many years, we had to give up the Newcastle clinic which, again, I regretted as I always think of patients as part of myself. Luckily, patients from that area could still go to the Chorley clinic and, as I was still within travelling distance, I could see them there from time to time. I was sometimes also available to give people free advice while consulting in health food shops.

Auchenkyle became busier. I was well aware that some people had to travel from very far afield to get advice and, although I tried to introduce other practitioners, people still wanted to see me personally, possibly because of the many years I had been in practice. Auchenkyle grew very quickly and, after we introduced additional practitioners, it actually

became too busy. At that particular point, when we really were at our peak, I received a visit from two important people from Holland who said that the time had now come for me to prove the efficacy of alternative medicine integrating with orthodox medicine. The Dutch Government had given a lot of money to aid this project and I was asked to work on it with the Dutch health service. It would be a great sacrifice to draw back from all my work in Britain, so I decided to do this part of the time and still keep on my clinics in Harley Street, Chorley and Auchenkyle, and allow about 70 per cent of my time to be taken up with the project in Holland. I looked into it and had a few talks with the Dutch health service, who were very interested in what I had to say, and we then started to plan a project of double-blind tests on patients who had osteoarthritis and rheumatoid arthritis. This would be monitored by one of the Dutch universities.

The project meant that my wife and I had to live in Holland and, fortunately, we managed to find a wonderful place near to where these trials had to be conducted. Right under the bridge featured in *A Bridge Too Far* was an estate (where my grandmother used to work as a nanny) overlooking the beautiful River Waal, in one of the nicest parts of Holland. The house, called Rozendal, had a rich history and still retained a lot of its original seventeenth century features, including a thatched roof, and it had a beautiful big pond at the foot of the hill. The minute I saw this house, full of character, I knew it was the place for us. My wife was over the moon about it and so the deal was done – we would live there and I would work on this research project to convince the orthodox medics that alternative medicine really worked.

An old monastery, set in over 300 acres of woodland, in which over 200 monks used to live, was offered to us as the

perfect place to carry out the research. The buildings were ideal and, on the ground floor, there was the biggest kidney dialysis centre in Holland. We were very lucky to find an underground source of water that had beneficial properties for rheumatic and psoriatic patients. This was a most nerve-racking experience. It was known that there was water there, but digging deeper and deeper cost a lot of money. The manager nearly gave up, but after much blood, sweat and tears came success. After a long time, the water, which was like gold, was found. The minerals in this were so rich that a big thermal bath was built, which was also beneficial for our project and we started work. Professor Mazek, a very well-known rheumatologist who was completely against alternative medicine, headed the orthodox part of the project, while I headed the alternative part. It was most interesting that each time he came to lecture me about diet, etc., he seemed to become more fascinated. It was total ignorance on his part (and that of his wife, who was also a doctor) that made him doubt my work, which I have so often found to be the case. However, we did work very well together. The professor also worked in a nearby hospital. We compared a lot of notes and, next to a room with his patients, I also had a room with other patients. The health service invited me to conduct several lectures and to set up and monitor the development of the patients. In the first few weeks, the professor's section of patients got better much quicker than mine, but as time went on, my patients became much more pain free and, whilst his patients still had very limited movement, mine were much freer. He was very impressed and the orthodox team became more and more interested in what I was doing.

I loved this work, but I was very unhappy in Holland. I could not forget Britain – and especially Scotland – where my

friends were and I was so happy each time I went back. We undertook a lot of important work in Holland, laid the foundation for these trials, which I am still happy about, and helped to build this tremendous place Klein Vink, into a centre of excellence in Holland where patients can not only find relief for their aches and pains, but also regain health and vitality. The work we put in there has certainly been valued. Professor Mazek and his team became impressed to such an extent that his wife, who was also a doctor, wanted to work with me. What started as a very difficult relationship ended as a great friendship, and, although I was sorry to leave there, I had to tell them that I wanted to return to Scotland. On one return visit I remember being so homesick that, on the road to Troon, I stopped in Johnstone, where I used to work with Dr Sarah Marr in her practice, also with a lot of rheumatic patients. I just wanted to be there for a little while until my feelings of homesickness diminished. I was always happy during the times that I worked in England and Scotland in between my research work in Holland and that is the reason I carried on there for nearly seven years.

Luckily, I managed to convince my daughter and her husband to come to Scotland, where Dr Tan could take over my practice and, when the new Bioforce was built in Irvine, the two businesses complemented each other. Overall, this exercise has been of great benefit; I have learned a lot, and we have worked together a great deal. One cannot argue with results, as was proved to my orthodox colleagues in Klein Vink.

One day, a big Bentley drove up and out stepped a very important minister from another country flanked by two bodyguards. He came in and sat down. He was dying of a tumour in his throat and began to tell me a quite remarkable story. He had been to the dentist for some work on a tooth.

After leaving the surgery, he had felt something in his throat. He had gone back the following day and the dentist had had a look at his throat, but could not find anything. He did nothing further for about two or three weeks. However, as he felt there was still something in his throat, he returned to the dentist who still could not find anything but advised him to go to his doctor. The doctor had a look, but could not find anything either. Nothing was found when the man returned a second time. Time went on, but he still felt there was something in his throat so he went back to the doctor who then sent him to an ear, nose and throat (ENT) specialist, who could not find anything either. Although the country he came from is very advanced in medicine, they could not get to the bottom of his problem – the ENT specialist even suggested that the problem was in his mind, and he should see a psychiatrist! He went to a psychiatrist, who told him that he was absolutely normal. He was then sent back to the hospital. More extensive tests were done and, by that time, because of the months that had elapsed since he first complained of the problem, a tumour had formed. He was told that if they operated, he would be left with no voice.

Disgusted, he looked for alternatives, and a friend, who was the president of a large car company and also a patient of mine, recommended that he came to see me – and here he was. I looked at him and could immediately see how distressed he was. I then proceeded to carry out a few tests. The dermatone tests showed up heavy metal, which made me think that there was a little truth in his theory about the dentist. I phoned the hospital where my friend Professor Mazek worked. We had a look and felt that the problem must have originated from a piece of amalgam which had come out of the tooth and lodged itself in the throat, where the cancerous process had started. I

was told this was a very clever diagnosis but was asked what could be done about it. I took the man in hand, treated him and successfully managed to dissolve the little piece of amalgam, after which his tumour disappeared. The evidence is clear – he still holds a very important position and, throughout his treatment, continued to carry out his very responsible job successfully. A lot of orthodox doctors were impressed when they heard his story. He later invited me to dinner, along with his friend (the car company president). That was probably the best dinner I have ever had, because it had been such a remarkable recovery. When I thought about this situation, I realised that one sometimes has to be a detective to figure out what can be wrong with a patient.

❧ ❧ ❧

Auchenkyle is indeed a lovely place. When we finally managed to get the gardens into order after the ruination caused by the previous owners, it became a very happy place. It took a lot of work to repair all the damage that had been done in the house. I am quite sure that the Frasers, who lived there for over 50 years, would have been proud of the restoration that took place. We then managed to buy the lodge house at the end of the road, which made the whole business complete. We also opened a wonderful little coffee shop. This has been a very welcome place for patients, who sometimes have to wait a long time. Many people will remember the great party we had in a marquee, set in the gardens, to celebrate my 25 years of being in practice in Scotland. People came from far afield – even from San Francisco, India, Sri Lanka and many other countries. This was a great event and now that I am reaching almost 45 years of being a practitioner, I look back

appreciatively at the experiences that life has given me.

We have such a wonderful job. I remember a time while I was working in one of the GP practices, when the senior doctor confided in me that he had a young doctor working there who was very miserable. Because I was older, he asked if I could talk to her. I will never forget that experience because it reminded me very much of the fact that being in practice means 'service above self', and that this is not a job, but a calling. She was constantly so unhappy that all the other doctors did not know what to do. As I passed her room, I noticed her gazing miserably straight ahead. I went in to see her and asked her what was wrong. She answered, 'Nothing.' I commented that she looked very unhappy. 'None of your business,' was her reply. I said, 'Well, that is not really an answer – why are you so unhappy?' She then opened up to me. She said she had been on call a lot of weekends, sometimes being called out for nothing, often having to deal with difficult patients and nagging people – she just hated the job. I asked her why she had chosen to become a doctor if she hated it. 'None of your business' was the answer again. I then told her that I had been in practice for many years and that some of my sons-in-law were also in practice – in fact, she might know one of them, as he could have been at university at the same time as her. She then started to take an interest and realised that indeed she did know him. I told her that he was very happy helping others in the course of his work, but if she was not happy doing this job, then she would be better to give it up. She was still quite withdrawn, but I persevered and had a very good chat with her. By the time we had reached the end of our talk, I think she had changed her mind. Some of the other doctors asked me what I had done, as they said she was a different person after I had spoken to her. Sometimes in life

you need to give things a little shake to realise what a wonderful job you have. If it becomes boring or a burden, then you know there is something wrong. I have always loved the word 'enthusiasm'. One dictionary gives its meaning as 'God in you'. If we are grateful for the life that we have and the creation we are part of, and can fill a little place, then things will be all right.

✺ ✺ ✺

Auchenkyle kept growing and we treated patients from every corner of the world. Sometimes I am amazed when I look back at the work at the clinic that has been done to help alleviate human suffering, at the gifts that all of us have been given and how we have made use of these in helping other people. I was very grateful that others, especially my son-in-law, kept Auchenkyle going during the seven years I had been away in Holland. Although it was hard to leave the beautiful place in which we lived and the interesting job I had done there, I was happy to be back with my own patients in Scotland and that encouraged me to work even harder than I was already doing.

New treatments were developed and, because of the media attention we received, we needed to expand further afield in order to cope with demand. In order for us to reach most people who wanted help, we decided to create some new clinics, so that a lot more could be done to help those who needed it. When we bought the building in Ayr to transform into a clinic, I remember how much work had to be done to restore the property, which is now a wonderful clinic for people to come to for a variety of different treatments. It is the same with our Edinburgh clinic. Located in a prominent position in York Place, this clinic is also doing well. Later on,

we opened one in Glasgow and, again, this great old mansion has been restored and is now a place where many people help to heal others. We also have affiliated clinics in the north of London, in Wheelton, and in Belfast. We have a total of ten clinics now, all with the aim of helping those in need. The Belfast clinic, which sometimes has a waiting list of three years for new patients, has been a great success. During the Troubles, I kept consulting there. It has certainly not gone unnoticed by me that many degenerative diseases and other illnesses developed in people there over the many years that the conflict went on. I saw the same when I opened the Dublin clinic. The enormously rapid growth of the economy there has affected people by causing stress and an inability to cope with these quick developments. It has left its mark on many people because they are constantly living with pressure, and have therefore paid the price for the rapid economic growth.

It is wonderful that I am able to travel to all the different clinics. Sorting out the misunderstandings the public and press have had about my work, and working towards integrating alternative and conventional medicine into a complementary system, have been difficult tasks. The example of the Dutch complementary medicine system, and my experience of this, has certainly been of the greatest help. Today, there are still enough evidential papers to show how alternative and conventional medicine have slowly married and been very beneficial to patients' health. However, the path towards a complementary system was not easy and, in the next chapter, I shall share a few good and bad experiences, and some interesting cases.

CHAPTER TEN

Healing Instead of Blundering

I once met Her Majesty the Queen of Great Britain at Holyrood Palace, and she told me she believes that it is most important for people in this country to have freedom of choice. This is a statement that has been made by many, but Her Majesty has a very open mind. With enormous intelligence, she has studied many subjects and, during the conversation that I was allowed to have with her, I was surprised at her wide knowledge of many forms of complementary medicine. Over the years that I have been working in this field, I think the most difficult part of my job has been talking to people with totally closed minds, who think that salvation is only to be found in orthodox medicine. I have a great respect for orthodox medicine and, as I have always said, what would we do without it? Nevertheless, it is great to have an open mind, at least to study the evidence and the efficacy of this tremendous subject.

Well over 200 years ago, our national poet, Robert Burns, wrote to Dr Moore, the well-known doctor and author of *A View of the Causes and Progress of the French Revolution*. This letter is very interesting to read. Basically, what he said is that

the blunders and mistakes we make are through ignorance. I have come across this ignorance many times while lecturing to students and postgraduates. I remember giving a lecture once in a hospital where there were a lot of young student doctors. At that time, evening primrose oil was very much to the fore and one student ridiculed its properties. I asked him if he knew all about it and he shook his head. I told him that I had read of the benefits of evening primrose in books from the sixteenth and seventeenth centuries and, today, I have also seen through evidential trials how much evening primrose has to offer us. It is always a problem when one closes one's mind to something that might be of benefit in the future. In the last chapter of this book, I will discuss a few people who were thought to be complete nutcases and whose views were completely discredited, but who are highly esteemed today. Copernicus, when his views of the solar system became known, was also thought to be a nutcase in his own time, yet we still believe today that he was right.

When I think of the few extraordinary cases where it has been shown that healing was possible and blunders have been made, they were probably the result of a closed mind.

A short time ago, when I was working in Northern Ireland, a young girl appeared with her father, mother and both grandfathers and grandmothers. They actually came to thank me for the miraculous recovery of this young seventeen-year-old. A month earlier, her father had phoned the clinic from the hospital to ask if I could see his daughter. He said that they would bring her by ambulance as she was almost dying. I very seldom say 'yes' because of my busy practice, but somehow my intuition told me that I should see her, and so, the girl arrived. She could walk, but I saw straight away that her centre of gravity was very much out of line. I also noticed that her

breathing was very heavy. I did my Chinese facial diagnosis and realised that this girl was indeed seriously ill. I asked her to lie on the bench and went to a certain spot right on the end of the gullet. It was actually quite obvious that that was where her problem was and, although she had had endoscopies and all kinds of tests, they had not found anything wrong and her parents were told that unfortunately she could not be helped as the doctors felt it was probably all in her mind. I used a very simple technique that I learned from Gonstead in the United States many years ago. He was a genius in bone symmetry and, by outwardly looking at the patient, could see what was out of line. The end of the gullet was almost bulging in this young patient and her rib cage was very much out of alignment. This procedure took me no more than three or four minutes in itself and I could then immediately see that this girl could breathe properly again.

Technically, she was in a very bad state. I told her father and mother that it wasn't in her mind, but there was a mechanical problem, and we could only hope and pray that this would be rectified. I sent her back to the hospital and asked her to eat very slowly and to have very small meals as I was not completely sure, without carrying out further tests, that she did not have a small hiatus hernia. She went back to the hospital and by the Monday she was much better. By Tuesday, the doctors who had seen her previously came back to look at her and they were quite surprised. By Wednesday, a professor came with some young graduates to see her and, in the presence of her parents, he told the young students, 'Here we have a typical example of a placebo. This girl had nothing wrong with her. It was all in her mind, but she went to a man who knows nothing about medicine. He did something with her and suddenly her mind told her that she was better.' Her

father said, 'That is not true, because if you had looked at her chest, you would have seen that she was completely out of alignment and, mechanically, this man put her back into the right posture.' The professor smiled. When the father asked him why he could not have done that, he just walked away with his postgraduates, still of the opinion that this was only a placebo. How often have I seen over the years that that was not the case: people with slipped discs and even a prolapse of the intervertebral disc have told the same stories. It has taught me to be very careful what I say without knowing the truth of the matter. Only when we can honestly say that we have looked at a case from every angle can we be justified in making a statement.

I never like to mention names and adhere to strict confidentiality. I sometimes see doctors, especially complementary ones, mention famous names when they advertise. I can honestly say, unless the patient has requested this, I have never done so. One evening a very well-known Scottish footballer came in to my clinic with his trainer, who had persuaded the player to see me. He was one of Scotland's best and greatest footballers. At that time, I treated players from Celtic and Rangers, and also a lot of players from the English teams. This man was a much-admired footballer and I could see in his face that he was very worried about something. He had already undergone a few operations on his foot and the professor in question had told him that he would never play again. This, for him, was a huge shock. He then developed diabetes, which made things even more difficult – being diabetic myself, I can understand why, because of the terrible worry and the emotional slap in the face of having been told that he would never play again, he had developed the disease. His trainer, who many people knew and who often

asked me to mention his name if I wished, Jimmy Steele, was a great Celtic supporter and, before he died, he left his training suit to me. I had a good look at the player's foot and told him I would deal with it. I gave him acupuncture treatment with moxibustion, and also helped with his diabetes. He got so much better that after three treatments he started to play again. After the sixth treatment, he went to see the professor, who was absolutely furious and threatened me with legal action if I let him play, saying I was very irresponsible. I told him that I could see no reason why he could not play. He went on to become the club captain, and played better than ever before for many years after that. This is a good example of the importance of an open mind.

It is not always easy to help certain people when they have been told they will never recover, because their hope has been taken away. This reminds me of the case of a girl from East Kilbride who came to see me in a wheelchair. She was definitely a multiple sclerotic patient and I am the last person who would say they can 'cure' multiple sclerosis. You cannot – what is dead is dead. What I will say, however, is that one can control it. I do not know what caused this to happen but, on this girl's second visit, after I had given her some acupuncture treatment, as she was coming off the bed she told me that she felt some strength in her legs. On that particular day, I had not used the needles by the book. I had taken a completely different route. I asked her to hold my hands and see if she could stand, which she did. I then asked her to try and walk a little. Of course, she was very weak, and her muscles were also weak as she had not been walking for a long time, but she felt she could. She then went home. Three weeks later, I saw her sitting in the hall. I asked my assistant, Teresa, to look and see if her wheelchair was in the cloakroom.

Naturally, I thought it was quite strange that she was sitting there without it. When Teresa came back and told me that there was no wheelchair there, I then called her name and, to my great surprise, she walked into the consulting room. Naturally, she was very happy and told me that she had experienced great benefit following the previous treatment and felt that she could walk again. On the fourth visit, she felt the same – until she had a visit from her neurologist. Her doctor, who was most surprised by her improvement (and has since sent quite a number of patients to consult me) had called the neurologist to see her. He was equally interested. He looked at her, then told her it was a welcome short remission and added that all he could do for her was to order her a chairlift, as she would soon be back in her wheelchair again. She was very distressed. A week later, she had regressed and could not walk, and had come back to see me. I sat her down. She was quite a religious lady, so I had a short talk with her, related a little bible story about people who have no faith and, even worse, people who have lost their faith, not only in themselves but also in others. I told her that, because of her faith, she should not think negatively but be positive in her mind about walking again and, luckily, she did. She is now serving behind the counter in her husband's shop and feels a lot better than she ever did before.

It is wonderful to think of the power of nature to heal people. If you give nature a chance and stay positive – which is always very important – it can be done. It is also important that one accepts professional advice and does what is recommended. Experience has taught me what is right and what is wrong, and patients can improve by taking their doctor's or practitioner's advice, as they are doing their best to help the patient.

A very famous singer, probably one of the most famous in the country, came to see me once in Harley Street. She told me that, unfortunately, she had problems with her singing, which had deteriorated and, because of this, she had become very depressed. In talking to her, I could see that she had problems with the right side of her jaw. I asked her if she had been to the dentist recently and, indeed, she had. She told me that after seeing the dentist, she had experienced some problems. In a matter of seconds, I adjusted her jaw, which had been causing tremendous pressure on the tempero-mandibular joint. If pressure is there, it always affects the hyoid bone, which can affect speaking and singing. That was exactly what had happened in this case. I treated this lady very quickly, and she looked at me with great disbelief, wondering how this could have helped as she was in and out the door within five minutes. After a week, she phoned me to say that her singing had improved very much and her jaw felt a great deal better. She wondered whether she should come back and see me or not. I told her that I would like to see her once more to examine her and hopefully find that everything was all right. And it was. She is still singing and a lot of people in this country still enjoy her beautiful voice.

Another story comes to mind, this time about a lady who is related to royalty. She came in to the clinic and told me that she felt very ill. I could smell candida. My extra sense, my intuitive sense, may have helped develop my breathing and sense of smell. This is a gift that perfumers are partially gifted with. When I smelled this candida, I knew that she spoke the truth – she was indeed ill. A lot of people think they have candida, but not all of them actually do. It is a yeast parasite that lives in all of us but is not always active. I told her that I wanted her to give up five foods – wine, cheese, mushrooms,

yeast and sugar. She answered that she would omit four of them, but she would not give up her bottle or two of wine a day. I said, 'Then I am afraid I cannot help you.'

'I will show you that I can do it,' she said. After six weeks, she came back and the same candida smell was still evident. After the second visit, I told her not to waste her money and she said, in no uncertain terms, that I was a lousy practitioner and she was going somewhere else. Some time later, I got a letter from her, saying that she had gone to a doctor in America who allowed her to drink her daily quota of wine and he had cleared her candida. In other words, I was not a good practitioner – she just wanted to let me know this.

Half a year later, there she was back before me. I said to her, 'Let me have a little look in your eyes first of all.' As I was looking with my iridology apparatus, she told me that she did not believe in such things and this was not a scientific piece of equipment. Nevertheless, I looked into her eyes and asked her where her left kidney was. She asked if I had second sight. I said, 'No, I don't have second sight at all. I see in your left eye that there is no left kidney.' She told me that 27 years previously her left kidney had been removed. That gave her a bit of confidence in my ability. She told me that although she had spent thousands and thousands of pounds going to this doctor in America, who promised that he would get rid of her candida, it had returned and, this time, she would be willing to cooperate with me. I asked her to promise to do as I told her, and she did. Luckily, I got rid of the candida, after which the other doctor in America got a letter from her saying that *he* was a lousy doctor!

There is another case that I shall not easily forget. In front of me sat a beautiful princess. I could see that she had many problems and a lot of misunderstanding in her life. I agreed

that, in her position, it was very difficult to work out what was the right thing to do. Her life was full of emotional ups and downs and she had to consider her position and the publicity she received, so it was difficult to advise what was best. Mistakes had been made by her advisors and others in the past. All that this girl needed to find the harmony within was understanding and compassion. But it is not always easy, and advice is not always appreciated. What worried me was that I sensed the way forward would not be a path of roses and instantly felt that she wouldn't have a long life. This decided me, at that time, to write my book *Inner Harmony* which, from all the letters I have received, has been of comfort for many. Patients have the right to confidentiality and therefore it is difficult for me to talk in depth about this case.

I also remember a duke who came to see me. He was so engrossed in his own health problems that, although he could easily have led a full life, he spoiled it by thinking of himself all the time. Every time he visited me, he talked and talked about all the terrible treatments he had received, the blunders that had been made in his treatment and wondered why his health never improved. I told him that the key to his own recovery was totally within himself but I couldn't open his mind. One day when he came to see me, I asked him to sit down and listen to me. I told him about the situation I had seen as a child, with the factory workers back in the cigar factory in my birthplace of Kampen, about the poverty of the people, followed by the Second World War and the tremendous suffering I had seen. I must say he listened intently. After I had finished, he said a very wise thing that showed he had changed his way of looking at things. He said that, while listening to my story of suffering, he realised that his problems were minute in comparison to the suffering I had

seen in my life. I was happy when I later heard that he had
got married and had something else on which to focus his
attention, instead of thinking about himself all the time. How
often do we see that, when people have too much money or
time on their hands, they become so self-important that they
forget to think of others, and to share. This is so important
and something I learned from Mother Teresa when I worked
with her in India. I once shared a platform at a conference in
Bangalore with the Dalai Lama and Mother Teresa, and we
had a wonderful talk. In our own ways, each of us was thinking
about love and sharing it with others, trying to do what we
could to help others. This is what life is all about and I always
come back to my war story when, on seeing the utter misery,
death and destruction, I promised God that I would share my
life with others to the best of my ability. This is one of the
most important things in life. One can get so involved in one's
own problems that one does not see reality any more.

This reminds me of a girl who came to see me, telling me
she had MS. I asked, 'Why do you think you have MS?' She
said, 'Because one doctor thought I might have.' I did a
Chinese facial diagnosis on her. This is something I often do.
It has helped me tremendously in my busy practices, and has
never failed me. Outwardly, the diagnoses are sometimes so
clear as to where the problems lie and, in this case, I saw that
this girl did not have MS. I asked her if she had had a lumbar
puncture. She said, 'No, but I have had MRI scans and some
white patches showed up.' So I told her that white patches can
also indicate an ME patient, and that I personally did not think
she had MS. She had imagined the pictures so well and had
even adopted certain MS symptoms that she had read about.
The mind is stronger than the body and the body will be
obedient to the mind. This is very often the root of the

problem. I then said to her, although I do not approve of it, that she should have a lumbar puncture to make absolutely sure. After she had the lumbar puncture, the doctor told her that indeed there were no indications that she had MS. This still did not convince her that she was healthy because she was now afraid that she couldn't have children. I sat her down and had a real chat with her, until I finally managed to convince her that she did not have MS. Once that penetrated her subconscious mind, she realised that I was right and improved from that day.

Often this happens with people who imagine that they are not capable of certain things and cannot do what others can. This reminds me of a very well known and much-loved BBC personality. For a long time she had tried to have a baby, but her subconscious mind told her that she could not conceive. I asked her husband and herself to come and see me. We had a long chat and there was absolutely no evidence on either side that this was not possible – he was perfectly all right, his sperm count was OK, motility OK, he hadn't had mumps; everything was fine. She was a very healthy woman, had no endometriosis, no other problems, was not too old to conceive, not overweight – everything pointed to the fact that they could have a baby. My intuition told me that they would conceive, and I am very happy to say that they now have two children and are the happiest family I deal with. In fact, their photograph is with me in my room to remind me that positive thinking is much better than negative, and it is a good idea to replace a negative thought with a positive thought and to say to oneself, 'I can do it.'

My dear mother always said, '"Cannot" lies in the cemetery and "will not" is its neighbour.' It is very important that we are positively minded in order to reach our goal.

The medical world is strange. Sometimes you need to be a detective to find out what is wrong with patients, sometimes you have to be a philosopher and, at other times, you have to use psychology to make your patients better. I once got a phone call from a doctor who had heard about me and the success we had at Roode Wald, our clinic in Nunspeet, from a colleague in Holland. She said she was very fond of one of her female patients, but she was also very worried about her because she could not walk, and medically there seemed to be no reason for this. I felt that she should come into the clinic to be examined and have tests. Perhaps by administering an acupuncture treatment I could do something to help. The lady was brought in on a stretcher and was taken straight up to one of the rooms. I had a good chat with her, tested all her reflexes and everything else I could think of, but could not find any reason for her paralysis. As it turned out, a psychological trauma was the cause. I felt it would be dishonest to give this lady a lot of treatments as I sensed that psychologically there was something far wrong with her. I gave it a lot of consideration and remembered an old professor I used to work with in Holland, who had a lot of ideas on dealing with patients with psychological problems, and I hoped that one of them would have the desired result in this case. I went to the health food shop, where I found a very big tablet called Ge Vee Tabs – only a vitamin pill! Then I returned home and told the lady I had found a tablet that could be the cure. I said I would give her this before she went to bed and that the next afternoon we would both have a walk through the garden, as her paralysis would be gone. This filtered through from her subconscious to her conscious mind, taking away the thought that was absolutely cemented in her mind that she could not walk. I prayed very hard that this would work, and the pill did

its job. The following day at 2 p.m., I asked her to take my arm so that we could walk and, indeed, we walked round the garden. That particular lady has been walking ever since. Once a thought has become a reality in someone's mind, it often becomes so deeply ingrained that it is very difficult to remove unless it is replaced positively. That was what I managed to do with this lady and, of course, she stayed with us for a while to make sure that she did not regress. After having been brought to Mokoia on a stretcher and then going back home walking, she told everybody how wonderful the treatment had been and even today, 30 years later, we have a lot of patients from that part of the world who remember the miraculous recovery of that patient.

The mind is stronger than the body and it is often important, when sudden thoughts are accepted by the mind, to break through the barrier to dispel any negative thoughts, replace them with positive thoughts and then wait for the results. It is quite astonishing the difference that even one word can make.

A very famous horse rider, well known as one of the best horsewomen we have in this country, was doing well in her career. Unfortunately, while she was in trials, the famous horse she was riding fell and she fell with it, quite badly. Both the horse and the owner were very badly hurt. The vet was called, who said that the horse would have to be put down, which would have been a crime. The master of the hunt advised the rider to come and see me. She phoned and asked if I could please see them. I saw them both and took them into treatment straight away. The rider advised me that the next week she and the horse had to compete in the world championships in Germany. This 17-hand horse and its owner had to be treated, and I made it my responsibility to help them. I saw them every

day. They went to the competition the week after, both well, and became champions. The pair won the championship in Germany. So, sometimes it can be done.

When trying to help others, it is very important that we keep an open mind and are not dogmatic or bigoted. On a very busy Saturday, a gentleman came in to Auchenkyle. He looked very worried and I could see that he was in distress. I asked him what was wrong and he told me that on Monday he had to have his leg amputated, as there was a cancerous growth in his knee joint. I looked at him and couldn't see any of the 10 outward signs of cancer (cancer often can be identified by 10 or even 12 outward signs), such as a dryness of the skin or damage in the mucous membranes. Although I didn't have a lot of time, I asked him to step on to the plinth so that I could have a look at his knee. My first thought was that this man did not have cancer. When I looked carefully at the knee, I could not see a lot of limitations. As we had our own asked centre, I phoned our radiographer, who worked daily in a cancer hospital, to take some X-rays of this man's leg and especially his knee, to find out if there was in fact a cancerous growth. I told him to go to our X-ray centre and the negatives were made. I asked the gentleman to come back in the afternoon to see me, by which time I would have the results of the X-rays. My radiographer phoned me and said that she had scrutinised the negatives, but couldn't see that there was anything to worry about – just a little arthritis in the knee. So I asked this gentleman if I could speak to his doctor. I phoned the doctor who was very unsympathetic. In fact, he said to me, 'Do you bl**** think you know any better than the hospital?' He was not willing to listen to my advice. I told this doctor, in no uncertain terms, that if no further X-rays were made in the hospital for this gentleman, I would hold him totally

responsible under the Human Rights Act for doing something that he shouldn't, and that seemed to do the trick. On the Monday, the gentleman went to the hospital in question. Another X-ray was made and, indeed, my radiographer had been right. The long and the short of the story was that the initial X-rays were from another patient and had got mixed up. It is quite frightening and it is often advisable to seek another opinion or a second diagnosis if there is any doubt about one's case. I never feel upset when people go for a second opinion. We can all make mistakes, although some are unforgivable. It is important to remember that we deal with life and life is very precious.

I saw a Rangers footballer not so long ago, who, like the player that I helped overcome a foot injury and diabetes, was in the depths of despair because he had suffered an injury which would put him out of the game. He had sought many opinions, none of which were the same. He was baffled. When he came over, I said, 'I will take you into treatment and prove to your coach, who has been very discouraging, that we will get your leg better.' His leg improved completely, but he could not get over the fact that he had been told that this injury was fatal to his career. It is therefore advisable to seek a second opinion before the door closes.

Often I feel that we have failed in medicine and, some years ago, when I did a talk in the House of Lords on some of my prison work, I made it very clear to the House that the importance of research is something that should have the full attention of the House of Lords and the House of Commons. I spoke about my work in male and female prisons. In female prisons, a lot of women are imprisoned because they have done something completely out of character due to a hormonal imbalance. They become like Jekyll and Hyde, and behave

irrationally. Because of that, they have committed crimes that they have deeply regretted – even to the point of murdering someone they dearly loved. A lot more focus needs to be placed on aspects of health that are easily forgotten, such as hormones and allergies. With one prisoner I treated, I studied his case thoroughly and looked at the five allergies he had, which had never really been investigated by doctors. Before he committed his last murder, he actually ate and drank the things that he was allergic to. Not only did these make him high, but they also caused him to do things that were totally out of character and which he now deeply regretted. In childhood, when he was naughty, he was probably given sweeties by his mother in order to keep him quiet. He is now a different character and, when Princess Margaret visited some time later, she asked him what had changed him. He said that he had now omitted all these foods from his diet, but before this he could even have murdered his guard. Now he wanted to change and to make up for all the things he had done wrong. He didn't ask her for his life sentence to be shortened. He asked her to understand that he now wanted to live differently. Other prisoners I have dealt with on this subject, where blunders were made in treating certain conditions and where healing has now taken place, have written a lot of letters to me stating that they only want to do better. There are cases that need further investigation and much more research. It is certainly of the greatest importance that we look at medicine and start at the grass roots. Where did things go wrong? Why did society fail to look at problems from a different angle? Life can be very sweet, but it can also be very bitter if it is full of misjudgements and misunderstandings, and loses its real purpose.

CHAPTER ELEVEN

For Goodness Sake

It is with real pleasure that I look back on the day I acquired my first little shop on Templehill, in Troon. I mentioned this occasion earlier but would like to say more about it now. We needed health foods for the clinic and, as the shop was very small and did not always have room to stock the goods we required, I had to go in quite often and ask the owner if she could order various things for me. She said, 'Well, this shop is really not something that I want to keep on.' I looked around and said, 'Well, what if we do a deal? I will give you £1,000 for the stock and £1,000 for the counter, the till and the chair.' Her face lit up and she replied, 'The deal is done.'

Nothing was further from my mind than running a health food shop and I intended to shut it down straight away. However, I did need the addresses of the suppliers so that I could order the foods that were needed for the patients at Mokoia. I went into the shop the next day to do the stocktaking and, amazingly, the stock came to just over £890, so my estimate was good and my intuition did not disappoint me. But here I was, landed with a shop that I wanted to close.

The next day, a very friendly lady, of whom I became very

fond, came to the door and told me that she often helped in the shop. She loved the customers coming in and offered them advice. Would I consider keeping the shop going? I said that I would give it some thought, and would meet her again that evening. As the weekly rent and rates were only £1 each, we decided to keep the shop open. Unfortunately, it only had a turnover of £40/45 per week. However, the lady in question was very keen, so I gave her some help in making the window look attractive to entice customers and the shop's trade began to grow and grow, until the premises became far too small and we had to start looking for larger ones. We found what we were looking for in Academy Street, a very big shop with lots of different goods, and things started to expand even further. The second shop I opened was in Kilmarnock, where the owner was too old to go on. The third shop to be opened was in Prestwick; the previous owners wanted to dispose of it. We expanded further by opening one in Largs, then Stranraer and later in Stewarton. Things mushroomed to such an extent that we eventually had ten shops. This reminded me of the time I had said, as a very small boy, to my mother, 'One day, mother, I will have at least ten shops.' Well, that was exactly what had happened, and it was really good fun. I remember one health food shop in particular which I didn't want to take over at all. It was owned and run by a farmer and his wife. However, they both went to a yoga seminar where his wife fell in love with the guru and the guru with her. She didn't want to come home and the poor man was then left with the shop. As he had a lot of work on his farm, he wanted to sell it. I phoned my marvellous right-hand man, Mr John McCallum, who was very loyal to me and we took over that particular shop.

We had completed quite a ring of shops in Scotland by that time. However, there was one shop we did not have; probably

the biggest in Ayrshire. We didn't know if this shop would ever come on the market until one day,' out of the blue, the owner and his wife came to see me and told me there was a chance they might sell out and wondered if we would be interested. However, in order to keep these shops trading and make them profitable, one needed a fairly big turnover. I listened and asked him what he was offering. To my great surprise, he took a Monopoly set out of his bag and put it in front of me. He then said, 'You have a lot of these – you even have Piccadilly Circus, but one shop that you haven't got is Park Lane – and I own that shop. We are offering it to you but, because it is Park Lane, we want a lot of money for it.' To cut a long story short, after protracted negotiations we bought that shop and to this day it still has the biggest turnover, although I don't actually own it any more.

That time holds a lot of fond memories, although we all had to work very hard to build the businesses up in the various towns and increase their turnovers. We had to introduce a lot of new items to sell in order to make them profitable. All the shops began to do well, however, especially the one in Ayr. I managed to get a baker to make certain breads to sell in the shops and, because of my days with the pharmacy, I also made remedies under our own name, which were very much appreciated. So everything was going absolutely wonderfully.

⚛ ⚛ ⚛

About 42 years ago, when I was in Edinburgh and not yet married, a relative of my wife had an extremely bad cough. I had two choices – I could go to a chemist, or I could go to a herbalist. In Bristo Place, I found a herbalist who had been trading there for decades. Although in those days the shop was

not very busy, it had certain customers who went there for remedies, so it was a blessing to many people. I went into that little shop, which was quite dark, but nevertheless very attractive with its brass knobs and smell of a real herbal pharmacy. Everything shone. What a delight it was! It reminded me of the *pharmacognosie* studies that I had to attend for my degree in Holland. I felt right at home in that little shop and was happy to talk to the herbalist, whose name was John Napier. He was a delightful gentleman who carried out his work with great enthusiasm, and when I told him I was a pharmacist, he was very interested in my work and also in my interest in herbs. I told him about Dr Vogel, of whom he had heard, and mentioned several of his friends who were in the same profession. We had a great talk. He prepared a wonderful prescription for me, which I gave to my wife's relative and, indeed, it helped her tremendously. I did not think for one minute that one day I would be the proud owner of that shop, nor did I realise how much it would come to mean to me.

It was many years later that the owners of Napier's, who by then were Gerard House, offered me the chance of taking over the business. I bought it from them lock, stock and barrel, not only because it had fascinated me so much all those years ago but also because of the recipes I thought I might find there. I took over the shop, renovated it from top to bottom and brought back the old philosophies of the Napier family who had operated this business since the seventeenth century. During those renovations, whilst breaking up a lot of the old cupboards which had degenerated over the years, I suddenly came upon a metal box full of real treasures, prescriptions that were used in the days of the plague and tuberculosis and all the different methods, plus a full book of remedies that had never been made. I felt as rich as a king. I saw remedies that

had been long forgotten, and the tremendous work that the Napier family had put into this particular place over the years in order to help others. What I had found was fascinating. I also came across the written reports of a court case. This was a big case that took place in Edinburgh concerning a man who had been drunk and had been brought in with a badly damaged eye, which old Mr Duncan Napier treated with a particular ointment. It wasn't until the drunk man had sobered up that he thought he would try to get money out of Mr Napier, claiming his ointment had caused damage to his eye. This was a big court case for those days, and the bills and the countless papers from the case showed how much it had all cost. Luckily for Mr Napier, at the end of it all, it was established that while the man had been drunk, he had damaged his eye himself and Mr Napier was totally exonerated because the ointment could not have caused any harm at all, nor was Mr Napier at fault for the way in which the man had been treated. Because of the publicity surrounding the case, this man actually made Napier's of Edinburgh very famous.

I built the business up as much as I could and started doing consultations there. I was very happy with Napier's, until the call came for me to go to Holland and work on the project to show the efficacy of herbal medicine. Then I had to sell the business, although I retained the premises myself as a reminder of the good times I had had running it.

I was involved in another fascinating find, when many herbs, long forgotten, were discovered at the site of a very interesting pharmacy in a medieval hospital. This was in the Soutra Hills just south of Edinburgh. Aerial photographs that had been taken of a certain area of the Soutra Hills suggested that some form of habitation had existed there. The photographs showed foundations buried on land where cows and sheep now grazed.

Excavations by archaeologists took place. The evidence showed that, in fact, there had been a medieval monastery on this site. In the twelfth century, the monks had provided a refuge and a hospital. When the English and Scots were fighting each other in the border wars, crossing the border at Jedburgh and then riding up to Edinburgh on what was known as The King's Road, they would come across this haven where they could be nursed and looked after medically before continuing on their journey. When the excavations started, Professor Brian Moffat, who was in charge of the whole operation, asked if I would like to go over and have a look at the excavation work. I felt very privileged to have been asked to be part of this and went along with my assistant, Teresa. We observed what was going on and were both very interested in what had been found. During the excavations, they discovered a church and, off to one side, what came to be recognised as an infirmary. A piggery was also discovered, almost intact, but the most interesting part for us was the area that had been used as a pharmacy, where they found herbs and prescriptions similar to those used at Napier's in Edinburgh. The pottery jars were the most amazing sight, with remnants of arnica, rosemary, skullcap, belladonna and all kinds of remedies that had been buried there since the twelfth century after the infirmary was burned to the ground. One fascinating discovery was the instruments that were used for bloodletting, and, even more interesting, a drain where layers of blood were still present after all these years. These findings were analysed in the laboratory and found to have traces of TB and typhus viruses present. In those days, after bloodletting the blood was disposed of in this large drain. Scientific analysis also showed the types of plants that were grown in that area at that time, many of which would have been used medicinally, such as flax,

mustard, barley and tormentil. It was amazing to see this whole operation taking place and to witness this excavation. I had a great desire to set up a museum there and Professor Moffat and I talked a lot about it. The cost, however, would have been too great, plus the purchase of the land would have been too expensive to make the whole operation profitable. So, today the cows are grazing again on what was a valuable and most interesting part of Scotland.

We could have called this site 'For Goodness Sake', after the great love and devotion of the monks. They did so much to aid the sick. We could learn from them: so much work and time must have gone into preparing those remedies, to help people who were stranded and needed help to enable them to continue on their journey.

❧ ❧ ❧

This was an interesting time. The whole health food industry, which was mainly based on good dietary management, herbal and homoeopathic medicine, started to spread across Britain very quickly. I carried out many lectures at various shops and associations and talked on radio and television, as I wanted to bring this matter much more to the fore. The health food industry started to grow very fast as people became more and more conscious of the benefits of organically grown foods. It was amazing to see the acceleration of growth in an industry that, at one time, was almost completely dead. I vividly remember the large health food manufacturers' exhibitions in the old days at the Royal Lancaster Hotel in London, which later moved to Olympia, and I followed these with great interest. Things were very different in Holland, where there were pharmacists, druggists and 'reform' shops, which

basically sold vitamins, minerals and trace elements, health foods, drinks and organically grown foods: health food shops in Britain showed a completely different picture. I was always amazed at how many people would turn up at the big lectures I held, especially in London. Many of them had a great desire to learn how to look after themselves, so they would ask a lot of questions. The public was beginning to realise the damage that could be done by E numbers, colourings and artificially grown foods that were sprayed with pesticides, herbicides or fertilisers.

When I worked in Teufen, I clearly remember Dr Vogel growing his herbal plants, trees and shrubs organically. These really flourished. Not so terribly long ago, I was given an example of the importance of good healthy foods, and investing in one's health. Many years ago, Dr Vogel planted two cherry trees. It is well known that cherry trees do not have a very long life. However, when I visited Teufen not long ago, it was interesting for me to see that after almost 40 years one of the trees was still alive. I asked the housekeeper, a very old lady, what had happened to the other one. Vogel had carried out an experiment with these trees. They had come from the same source and the same family. One of the young trees was planted in a small plot and artificial fertilisers, herbicides and pesticides were used to encourage its growth. He planted the other cherry tree further away from the first one, and grew it completely organically – it was fed organically and had no artificial manure. The first cherry tree bore fruit a lot quicker than the organically grown one. The fruit was also bigger and looked much better, but the odd thing was that it did not have the smell of a cherry. The cherries on the organically fed tree were not as big, they did not have such a wonderful colour, but the taste was gorgeous, and it had survived while the other

had died. Many times, Vogel spoke about those two cherry trees. As he always used to say, 'You get out of it what you put into it.' The same applies to the human body and, in the long run, you will have a longer life if you feed it well.

I thought about this when I was there some time ago on an excursion, taking people through the old place where I used to work and where my heart still was, thinking how hard we worked to prove to the world that those philosophies were right. The philosophies of Vogel, Napier and Mr Abbott of Leigh are still valuable today. People must realise that life is valuable and we only get out of life what we put into it. As for the cherry tree, which was looked after with care and devotion, it was almost impossible to believe that it was still alive after all those years. It reminded me again that I should instil in people that we live in a time when a strong immune system is extremely important.

Mr Abbott had a herbal practice in Leigh, Lancashire. He saw everything in black and white and would share his philosophies in no uncertain terms (and not always in the most friendly way!), as he was very keen that his patients kept to his rules. I only had the pleasure of meeting Mr Abbott once. I was very impressed with some of his patients who came to see me in the clinic in Chorley and, as I had heard so much about his work, I wanted to meet him, but never had an opportunity to talk to him. What I was most interested in was that Mr Abbott had a sort of black box in one of his rooms. It looked like an iron cage, with a little seat inside and a few monitors. At that time, I had no idea just how advanced Mr Abbott's vision was: he was working with electromagnets, whereby he could greatly improve his patients' energy. This was not just a diagnostic tool, although he also learned a great deal about his patients while they were undergoing treatment.

Never did I think over 30 years ago, when I first saw this place, that I would ever become the owner. Mr Abbott, who had been married four times, had a great history. Growing up in a coal-mining area, where there was a lot of TB and chest problems, he started to search for ways in which nature could help him. When he discovered all the things that natural medicine had to offer, he started to study as a herbalist. He was a very clever man, and the books and recipes I found in that clinic are of the greatest value and are greatly treasured. Mr Abbott was very studious, which was why his practice was so big. People would come from as far away as London and beyond to his herbal practice in Railway Road. He was an active man but, unfortunately, due to a tragic accident when he was quite elderly, his life came to an end, which was a big shock for his patients, as he had helped so many. He too was misunderstood. He was threatened with prison and had a court case brought against him by a patient who wanted to sue him unjustifiably. Thankfully, like Mr Napier, the verdict was in his favour and he was acquitted.

It is very important in life that whatever we do, we do it honestly. I remember my mother often said, 'You never need to worry about anything as long as whatever you do is done with honesty and dignity.'

Mr Abbott's recipes were even better than Napier's. His concoctions went a lot further and when I found his treasury of recipes and other things he had left behind, I counted myself the luckiest man in the world to have these in my possession. Today I still own Abbott's of Leigh, and people all over the country are helped by his recipes, which were long forgotten but have now been resurrected for the good of many.

❧ ❧ ❧

It was a wonderful industry to be involved in. Through the media, knowledge about health food shops, herbal shops and herbal clinics became much more widespread and popular. Why was there such a huge interest in alternative health at that time? Personally, I think that people were growing concerned about the side effects of drugs and if they felt they could improve their health naturally, then they were very happy to do so. During my travels, which I shall speak about in the next chapter, I have been in many health food stores throughout the world and consulted there. When I think of Mrs Gooch's health food stores in America, which were probably between 25/35,000 square feet, our health food shops in Britain seem like miniatures in comparison. The potential of those shops was enormous. I still remember, with the greatest pleasure, the times I consulted in Mrs Gooch's shops, especially in Hollywood and Wiltshire where I had consulting rooms, and where I saw some of the most famous film stars in the world. I would give them nutritional advice and remedies to balance their very busy taxing lifestyles. They frequently had little sleep and their bodies were screaming for harmony and nourishment. I was also encouraged by Sandy Gooch's desire to get this important message over to people and to make them realise how important this was. I helped with school excursions to the shop, and we tried to instil in the children how important it was that they looked after themselves, building an immune system for the future and the importance of good food instead of junk food. I was pleased that so many universities in the States had asked me to go and lecture on the importance of nutrition and health food.

Throughout my travels, I have been encouraged by seeing that people from all over the world now have an understanding of the things that I have been preaching about for so long. The

other day I read that cardiologists were advising people to eat six apples a day for their heart problems. This is a very positive step, but has come just a little too late. For many years, we have been preaching this particular gospel, knowing that we have a live body that needs live foods – not dead ones – to exist. The body needs 91 nutrients, and it won't get them from a synthetic pudding or a tin of tomato soup that has never seen a tomato. One message that I like to give is, for goodness sake, keep the body as healthy as possible. The outflowing aura that I often see in people, and which has been scientifically proven on the Kirlian photography machine, can also show whether food is alive or dead. If we look at a black and white photograph of a dead piece of meat, there is virtually no aura, but if the same is done with an organic apple or a piece of fruit, we see an almost unbroken energy aura. I am thankful for the gift that God has given me. When I see a patient in front of me, look at that outflowing aura and see the breaks and the holes, I feel it is my responsibility to try and mend them – for goodness sake.

My very loyal and excellent bookkeeper, Mrs Nancy Buchanan, and I have often thought about how we could serve people better and quicker. A new idea came to our minds, and we are now trying to encourage people to help themselves to better health with guidance and information, by setting up Jan de Vries Health and Diet Centres. The idea originated in Troon, where we had a health food shop called Jan de Vries Health and Diet Centre, which included a great information bank which people found helpful. The future Jan de Vries Health and Diet Centres will not only have remedy sections that are safe for people to use, but will also provide consultations where people can come and get advice. It is not always easy to find good practitioners, and I feel that these

centres are going to work very well. We have started in Glasgow, next it will be Dumfries, and so we will continue with this very specialised idea to bring this facility closer to the public. One important thing is that the growth of the health food industry must be controlled. Too many cowboys and charlatans have profited by exploiting this field, and that is not always to the benefit of patients. I sometimes see patients who have gone to see such people and have not been monitored while taking remedies. It is very worrying to see the effect this can have, and therefore it is very necessary that experienced people who have devoted their lives to helping others control the industry.

❦ CHAPTER TWELVE ❦

The Flying Dutchman

It has been a great privilege for me to have visited 61 countries over the years and lectured in 40 US states. Although this is a terrific honour, I have actually seen very little of these countries – mainly lecture halls and airports. The little I have seen throughout the world, however, is a real treasure to me. I often think back to the very heavy lecture schedules that I had, where I was sometimes travelling two or three times a day by plane from one place to another so that I could lecture and spread the message. When I get more time, I would love to see the places I have lectured in properly. Hopefully that will happen some day.

In the meantime, I have wonderful memories of the places I have been and, travelling through our own country, I have very much enjoyed and valued the villages, towns and countryside where I have given hundreds of lectures. Throughout Britain, I have admired the beauty of this country. Many of my memories go back to the days when audiences might vary from 10 or 12 people to thousands. I am terribly privileged to have made so many friends throughout the world during the course of my work. It would be impossible to list

all the places I have lectured, or all the good and bad bits of these travels. However, I will mention a few that spring to my mind and which I often think back to.

About 20 years ago I did a talk in Los Angeles in the Ambassador Hotel. Afterwards, a gentleman who later became a real friend of mine, asked me if I would go to Canada and give a talk in Toronto to a small group who had started an annual health conference called Total Health. I talked to him and, as we were both going to a meeting of the Rotary Club in Los Angeles, we shared a lot of ideas and, being on the same wavelength, I agreed to go. It was a most revealing meeting, with about 12 speakers, of whom I am now the only one left. Over the years, a lot of these wonderful people have passed away – people who worked so hard for the sake of health and gave up their lives to this work. Some of them mysteriously died, like my friend, Leon Shelly. It is still a mystery to me how these healthy people suddenly developed strange illnesses and died in the prime of their lives. Although I have my own suspicions, I am sure that in time we shall find out what really happened to them.

The conference in Toronto was wonderful, with 500 visitors, and I really enjoyed it. It was not without problems, though, as the Canadian authorities and drug industry didn't like the idea of some of the alternative treatments being promoted there. People like Max Gerson, Dr Mendelson, Dr Kelley and many others who spoke that night are no longer with us. They fought hard to bring the message closer to the people and I remember the last time I visited my friend Leon Shelly, who fought against pollution and against the establishment as it then was. A mysterious illness took his life. I think of Dr Mendelson, to whom I spoke on the Saturday evening after his brilliant lecture on medicine; the next day, after he left

Toronto, I phoned his daughter and was told that he had died suddenly. A host of questions surrounding these mysteries became a bit clearer to me when, on one of my visits, five minutes before I was due to go on the platform, by this time speaking to thousands of people (as Total Health had grown so fast by then) a letter was handed to me by the sheriff of Toronto. I was warned about what to say and what not to say, and told that if I did not keep to the rules laid out in that letter, I would be prosecuted. In other words, it would really be better if I didn't speak there at all. I went to my friends, Claus Schmidt and Hermann Geiger, and when I showed them the letter they said, 'Jan, what are you going to do?'

I said, 'I will speak. My mother taught me that when you have an honest message, you have nothing to fear.' I probably gave a better talk that evening than I have ever done before because this threat kept my adrenalin flowing. I believe in the freedom of speech. We had a most wonderful conference and I went back year after year.

On my travels throughout the United States, I have given talks, seminars and conferences in over 40 states, and spoken on radio and television. I have often met with opposition and been threatened with imprisonment and prosecution, but I have battled on. I remember that on one visit to St Catherine's, Canada, an interviewer kept me on air for two and a half hours, telling me that his programmes were listened to as far away as Buffalo in the USA and that it was important that I give people the message. In Vancouver, we built up a wonderful conference and it is with great respect that I think of the people who worked so hard to bring health to people in that beautiful part of the world. At one of the highest points in Vancouver, looking over British Columbia and Vancouver Island, the views were breathtaking and ones that I looked

forward to after very busy days. Gazing out over God's wonderful creation, I felt it was worthwhile tackling governments and health officials to keep this great world free of pollution and destruction.

In the United States, where I gave hundreds of talks and seminars, I met with a great deal of goodwill and a thirst for knowledge of what nature had to offer. I remember one morning having to go on television. It was in Portland, Oregon, and I was asked to give a talk on my book *Menopause*. I had been on television before with these particular interviewers, Jim and Mary, whose programmes had millions of followers. When I arrived, the drug industry had taken offence at a book I had written about food. Together with a few other carefully chosen people, they wanted to challenge me and attack me on the book I had written. When I had met Jim and Mary a year earlier I liked them very much. When I did an iridology on Jim's eyes, I asked him what had happened to part of his heart. In great amazement, he said to me, 'How do you know? I have had a heart bypass.' With Mary, I did a similar thing and asked her what was wrong with her neck as I saw problems there and that she had severe whiplash. Luckily, this couple were sympathetic and so we went on with the programme. The first lady who attacked me was sitting a bit away from me. She told me that she drank between four and six bottles of a special fizzy drink every day and felt very well on it; it also appeared to have cleared her asthma. Jim then asked me what I thought about this particular drink. I told him that it was a good window cleaner! Then I turned to a coloured lady and asked her why she was ill. She replied, 'I am not ill.'

I said, 'I think you are. From where I am sitting, I can see you are ill.' I used Chinese facial diagnosis. I said, 'Apart from

everything else, your hair is in a terrible state, your nails are breaking, your skin is deteriorating and you really have to seriously look at your diet. I would advise you to read my book on food.' I was quite happy with that particular book, as one of the big Sunday papers in Britain had given it a great appraisal and one professor who wrote about it said that it would benefit everyone's health if they read this book. So, I told her I would present her with a copy of my book and she should look seriously at her health. In front of us, there was a table full of junk food – and I mean real junk food. Mary lifted a sort of bun, called a Susi Q, off the table. Susi Qs were very popular in America at that time and Mary told me that the next lady ate two of these for her breakfast every day and felt great, as they contained a lot of zinc. I lifted up the Susi Q, with its layer of artificial cream in the middle and a red cherry on the top. I asked the lady if it was true that she ate two of these every day, and she said it was. I then asked, 'And why are you ill?'

'There is nothing wrong with me' was her reply. I said, 'Yes there is, you have rhinitis, sinusitis and I am sure you have allergies, as well as being grossly overweight.' She then nodded her head. Later on, that lady came to see me as a patient. The attack by the food industry on my book came to nothing.

At the end of the programme, Jim said that I was to speak again in Portland that evening. When I arrived at the place, there were so many people there that I heard one lady saying to another, 'It looks as though Elvis Presley has been resurrected. Who is going to be speaking here?' I ended up in a mall, a very large open place, with three microphones talking to people regarding their health problems – these people had an enormous need to get help.

In Chicago, I had a similar experience. When I arrived in

Chicago, at a pharmacy called Merz, a little bit of the United States's history was evident, as this was the oldest pharmacy and also lovely to look at. There was a big illuminated flashing banner draped across the street that read 'Jan de Vries is here'. The evenings were mobbed. They were wonderful experiences.

Going back to the days when Gaylord Hauser was alive, I remember a wonderful experience when he gave a very eloquent speech and I was due to speak after him. Gaylord Hauser was a health guru from America, who was not only greatly loved by the film stars, but was also a man who had the tremendous ability of getting his message across to the public. He was a picture of health himself, even when in his nineties. To continue with the story, I was extremely worried as I felt I could certainly not come up to his standards. I spoke for about an hour and my reward came later when a little man came up to the platform, put his hand on my shoulder and said, 'That was a wonderful Scottish accent this afternoon.' I told him that I was Dutch, but I was very proud of the fact that he could hear the Scottish accent in my voice and told him that lots of people in Scotland called me 'Mac Vries'. I have seen so many people in the health food markets – too many to write about in this book.

It was not always very easy as America is full of contrasts. Generally I met the most loving people, but there were exceptions. One afternoon, I was consulting in a very big store – 35,000 square feet – and, in the vitamin department some yards away, was the check-out assistant. Two men came in and demanded money, which he wouldn't give them. They then shot him, took the money and walked out. I was devastated because the poor man, who was only doing his job, was shot dead and the two men got away. Despite these terrible things, life has to go on.

Another lecture comes to my mind, this time in San Jose, in the US. It is a lovely place with beautiful scenery. I was at a big Jewish health food market. The owners had arranged that I should do a talk in the evening in a big hall belonging to the synagogue.

When we arrived that evening, the place was absolutely packed, but more and more people continued to arrive. When the rabbi came to listen to my lecture, he saw the crowd situation and said to me, 'You cannot hold all the people in here,' so I asked him what could be done. 'Well,' he said, 'you can use the synagogue if you are willing to put on a little cap and talk from the pulpit.' This was difficult because I am not Jewish. When I told him that I was partly Jewish, however, and had Jewish blood in me, his face changed and he said 'Well, that changes the picture. Put on that little cap and go ahead.' I never saw a place so full.

In Tampa, I had a similar experience, as again we had a big hall for the talk and, in the afternoon, I had talked to a lot of people in a big health food marketplace. Again, when we arrived in the evening, the place was crammed with people. When the minister came, he said that I could not have my talk there and what I really needed was the church. I asked him if he would be willing for me to use the church and he said that would be fine, but it might be better if I could incorporate something about the bible into my lecture. I said to him that I could probably speak a bit about herbs from the bible and he thought that was a brilliant idea. It was a talk that I enjoyed because I racked my brain to think of biblical herbs. That evening was such a success, especially when I mentioned the advice given in one of the oldest books of the bible, Ecclesiastes. In the last chapter there is a wonderful little story. It says that, as one gets older, one must remember the Creator

of youth. In Ecclesiastes 12:3–6, it tells us what happens as one gets older: 'the keepers of the house' (the legs) start to tremble, 'the grinders' (the teeth) become fewer, 'the windows become darkened' (the eyes) and 'the doors shall be shut in the streets' (our ears). Advice is given in some translations that one should look to the caperberry for help. In other words, the use of the caperberry will be beneficial when one gets older, when the memory (the golden ball) and the heart (the picture) start to fail. Everybody stormed in to the chemists and health food stores to find extract of caperberry, which was not there because, again, it is one of the forgotten herbs. It was a wonderful story and, along with all the other biblical herbs I mentioned, contributed to a great evening. However, this lecture had an impact on me and I felt I should investigate the caperberry. When I finally found the extract of caperberry (which grows profusely in Israel), I realised that indeed it was of great benefit, aiding vitality and energy and, following some research, I incorporated it into one of my flower essences.

Another time that I often think about was when I was asked in Miami to open a large store. I had to arrive quite early and, of course, I was dressed up to the nines for this big opening because a lot of people from the health food world would be gathered there. We had a most wonderful time. Two boys who were with me asked if I had ever visited Miami Beach. I told them no, I never had, and they said, 'Well, why don't we take some time off and go there?'

On a glorious day, when most people were lying half naked on the beach, I stepped between them wearing my Sunday suit, enjoying the wonderful sea views and experiencing the feeling of being on the sands of Miami Beach. Often, when I think of that occasion, I smile to myself and think, 'Will I ever be able to enjoy sunbathing on Miami Beach?'

In India and Pakistan, when I lectured and worked in one of the main hospitals in Bombay, I also had some wonderful times, although there are enormous contrasts in those countries. When I treated some of the richest and most important people there, it drove me to try and work hard for the Third World and to help those in need, not only financially but also with their health problems. I treated world leaders and was greatly supported by the Sumaya family, who were a great help to me in the course of my work there.

Back in the Scandinavian countries, I lectured, helped students leading up to their exams, visited universities and also the oldest medical library in Stockholm, where Dr Voll and I looked at records relating to original medicine. In the oldest department of books, it was recorded where medicine started. It is wonderful to see many aspects of healthcare returning to traditional treatments. Medical people all know about the Karolinska Institute. It is a marvellous medical library housing the most fascinating books. In the oldest part of that library, where there are thousands of books, one can read of old medical folklore from many centuries ago. We were especially interested to see that so much had been written on herbs, flowers, foods, barks of trees and leaves which were used in folklore for medicinal purposes. There was so much material contained within that library that we could spend years expanding our knowledge and it would be quite beneficial for medicine to inspect these old writings.

In Sri Lanka, where I worked during the revolution, in the Kaliboa Hospital in Colombo, I saw the most awful scenes, but it encouraged me that traditional or indigenous medicine was promoted by the government. I saw the oldest forms of medicine practised in Sri Lanka. When I sold a house and gave a lot of the money to this particular hospital for development,

I was sorry to see how some of that money was spent on erecting a statue and, with great honour, this was accepted. However, I would much rather have seen all the money being spent on medicine to alleviate human suffering. Nevertheless, great lessons were learned from what I saw in Sri Lanka.

From Sri Lanka, I went to Zambia, where I had to treat some of the most important people in the country. While there, I asked permission to see a few hospitals, which was granted by some of the leaders of that country, but I was shocked to see some of them packed with AIDS sufferers. It was heartbreaking to hear the cries of help from patients who were battling with an illness for which medicine had no answer. I had the privilege of staying for a little while in that beautiful country with its wonderful blue flowers along the streets.

When I left Zambia, I had the most horrific experience on the way home. We were told our plane was being hijacked. Luckily, everything turned out all right in the end, but the pilot had to land in a godforsaken place in Eastern Germany. When we landed, we were kept in the plane for six hours, where there was really no outlook at all, just a lot of nervous people. I managed to settle most of them down and kept the ones who were very nervous as calm as possible. It wasn't a scary business, except for the fact that no one knew what the outcome would be. Finally, after negotiations were finalised, we were allowed to leave and landed in Bonn. I ran for my life when I came out of that plane, and was so happy to see the British Airways desk. I asked them when the first plane to London was and was told that it would be in ten minutes. I managed to get a ticket and when the lady asked about my luggage, I said, 'Never mind the luggage. Let me go home.' I was so grateful to be safely back home again when we landed

on British soil. It was a shattering experience; sunshine and shadows were keeping life very interesting.

I had a very nice experience during one of my plane journeys, however. I was asked by a stewardess to go to the first-class section. I never usually travel first class because it is basically against my principles but, as I was very tired, I accepted her offer. I sat down, had a wonderful meal, and was treated to champagne and everything that she wanted to give me. Then she suddenly said, 'Do you not recognise me?' I looked at that beautiful girl, and she told me that my best friend had given birth to her back in Nunspeet and now lived in Switzerland. This was her daughter, who had treated me to such luxury. Her mother had told her about me, she recognised me from the photographs and treated me so well. This was one of the nice things that happened during my travels.

Another time, I was sitting in a plane with two ladies who asked me where I was going. I told them that I was going to Belfast. Then they asked me where I had come from. I told them from Scotland. They asked me if I knew Jan de Vries, who had such popular programmes with Sean Rafferty – they were desperate to meet him! I told them he was sitting beside them. This is an uplifting story that very often helped in the work that I was doing.

Dr Vogel once asked me to give a talk to medics in West Germany in a place called Freiburg. Because this talk had to be in German and he couldn't manage, he asked me to go. I enjoyed looking around that marvellous city with its universities and beautiful buildings before going to the big meeting, where I had to speak on viruses, allergies and the immune system. The talk went well, but as medics and students often like to criticise, or sometimes just be difficult,

one student started to question the excellent remedy called echinacea. Echinacea is a wonderful plant to help strengthen the immune system and I had already spoken about it. He was very difficult about it until one lady doctor stood up and said that she had been on holiday in Brazil and, during her holiday, suffered a bad throat infection which caused a swelling like a golf ball in her throat. She tried to find a pharmacy to get antibiotics, but instead found an old health food store that had one bottle of Echinaforce left on its shelf. She thought of getting some chamomile tea, but the health food shop owner advised her to try Echinaforce instead. She bought it and looked at the label, which read 'three times daily, ten drops'. She thought she would double that amount as she really didn't believe that herbal medicine was effective. She told the whole meeting that within three hours the abscess had burst and by the next day she was fine. She added that, as a result of her quick recovery, she was now very interested in homoeopathic and herbal medicine. She was most encouraging and a tremendous help to me at that meeting.

When I travelled from there, I had another very nice experience. The next day I had to leave for the United States and do a talk in one of the colleges on alternative medicine. After I had finished speaking, a vote of thanks was given by a nice young man. He explained that he had met me seven years earlier when I was giving a talk to students at the Naturopathic College in Toronto. He was taken there by a friend and had listened to me intently. The day after that talk, he was supposed to be buying a photography business in Toronto as he had just studied as a photographer and was quite well known for his photographic skills. However, after my talk, he hadn't slept all night. He had become so interested in the alternative remedies field that he went back to the college and

asked if it was possible for him to study this. He forgot all about his photography plans and booked himself into the college to become a naturopath. Today, he is one of the most famous naturopaths in the United States and that was the story he told when he gave me the vote of thanks after I spoke at that particular college. My heart was greatly warmed and I have always kept in contact with that particular young man, who now also writes a lot of books and is well known in Canada and America.

In South Africa, where I lectured in the main cities, I was criticised by a very well-known professor of pharmacology in Durban. I was to be interviewed by him, but I was wary about it as Earl Mindell, the man who wrote *The Vitamin Bible*, had returned following an interview breathing fire at the way the professor had attacked him. My anxiety wasn't helped by the fact that the evening before I had agreed to do an interview with black television. In those days, when apartheid was still rife, they didn't care much when I told them that we all have red blood and whether a person's skin is black, yellow or white makes no difference to me, as I see everyone as a human being. I was worried about this professor, as I knew he hated alternative medicine and was ready for a confrontation. I met up with him in the waiting room and I could see he took an instant dislike to me. Then he asked me where I lived. I told him in Troon, Scotland. 'Ah,' he said, 'where the famous golf courses are.' I said, 'Yes, and I live almost on Royal Troon golf course.' He told me he had played there. His focus immediately turned to golf and, when he heard that I had treated lots of famous golfers from around the world, he became extremely interested. We went on the programme and I can still hear him saying, 'Here is the most wonderful man who lives in my favourite place and with my favourite game –

golf.' After that, we got on famously together, discussing different topics relating to health. So that was another victory for me. Afterwards I treated myself by going to the beach. While I was going in and out of the water, I got a shock when I saw a notice stating that this beach was only for the black community. Not that it made any difference to me, but I was supposed to go to the beach for the white community. Incidents like that were very educational.

I had a very interesting case, again in South Africa, when I was staying with a homoeopathic doctor and her husband, who was a surgeon. I really enjoyed that visit as I had so much in common with her, and had some very lively discussions with her husband, as he was so against alternative medicine – and not without reason. He saw many patients who ended up in hospital very ill because they had consulted witch doctors. The couple had a chauffeur, a very nice man, who was fascinated by my ballpoint pens. I got friendly with him, but I could see he walked very badly (one of his legs was shorter than the other) and told him that I would like to help him to walk a bit better. He said absolutely no way, because he was going to the witch doctor. I gave him all my ballpoint pens and managed to persuade him to take me with him to the witch doctor because I wanted to see what he actually did. I have never seen such a painful and awful experience as that which my chauffeur friend, of whom I had grown very fond, had to endure. I asked the witch doctor if he could put the man's left and right legs into a certain position. He said, 'No problem.' He took a very hot poker and went to four points in the shorter leg and told the man that it was now balanced, but there was no difference. I showed him. I wasn't allowed to touch the patient, but it was obvious that one leg was still a lot shorter than the other leg, and I asked him to put the ankle

bones together so that I could show him. He then took a handful of wishbones, threw them in the air and prayed to his god to correct the problem, but nothing happened.

By luck, I had a few copper and zinc magnets in my pocket that I had taken with me, as I wanted to see this particular exercise working. In opposite directions, I put the copper and the zinc magnets on his sacrum, on the ileum and some on the left and the right legs. I too prayed very hard to my god, who never leaves or forsakes me, and is always with me. My prayers, in conjunction with the treatment, worked. One could almost see the left and right legs straightening themselves out. I asked the witch doctor which treatment he thought was best. He shrugged his shoulders and walked off. I am sure that my friend, the chauffeur, would still go back to him, as his belief in him was so strong. That was a nice experience that I shall never forget, and which I hold dear when I think of my visits to South Africa.

As I have said, it would be too much to write about all the countries I have visited and the many experiences I have had. I have been greatly encouraged by people's support. When I went to an enormous health food store in Richmond in America, a woman stood for a whole afternoon in a queue just to get my book *Do Miracles Exist?* When she finally got the book, I signed it and she told me that, as the queue was so long, she had had to wait four hours for her book. I expanded on this subject in *Do Miracles Happen?*, as I have often witnessed unexpected reversals in illness and disease through intervention. I have often asked myself in such cases whether this is divine intervention, or just coincidence.

In Cincinnati, I was greatly encouraged when a family came in with three children. I had been in that place about eight years previously and had first met this couple then. I

remembered them, and their photograph is with me on my study desk to remind me of the little miracles that can happen. At our first meeting they were both very upset and emotional as they desperately wanted a child. Nothing had worked; none of the doctors they had consulted could help them and it was driving them apart. They asked if there was anything I could do. I hadn't a lot of choice, so I went and collected four remedies. I gave them some advice and as there were no obvious reasons – except he had a low sperm count and she had irregular periods – I told them what to do. Now, eight years later, here they were with their three children; the first remedies I gave them had worked and, every time they wanted another child, they had repeated the procedure and it had worked. What a joy. On that visit my public relations man, Peter Rule, was with me. He was so amazed that he sent his daughter and son-in-law, who had the same problem, to see me and, again, they were successful in having a child. These little miracles are an encouragement to keep going.

❧ ❧ ❧

My travels also took me to Australia, which I dearly loved, as I spent my days lecturing at the Botanic Gardens in Sydney, Melbourne, Brisbane and Perth, and was especially pleased at the tremendous gatherings I had in Melbourne. Those days were absolutely wonderful. However, as I have said in so many of my lectures, man has three bodies, not one. They should all be in harmony and health is dependent on them all. The immune system is vital for the world we live in today. Unfortunately, on this occasion, I became very much aware of that fact. I was on my way to Australia for the third time, having just finished a very busy day at Harley Street. I was

tired. I had also received a letter which had greatly upset me. When I arrived at Heathrow Airport, I was told that the only available seats were in the smoking section, unless I went first class. As first class is against my principles, I had to sit next to a lady who was very nice but smoked all the way. To summarise, my emotional body had been attacked by the letter, my physical body had been attacked by the very busy day I had had as well as the cigarette smoke, and my mental body was under strain because of the short time I had to prepare for the lectures in Australia. So my three bodies were totally out of harmony. When I arrived in Melbourne, I had no time to have a rest, but had to go straight in to take a big lecture. The next day, we had to go into the bush, a very taxing experience as I had to speak on the characteristics and the signatures of plants, herbs, flowers and trees that I had never seen before but, by their signs, I could tell what they should be used for. As we had an entourage of reporters with us, I had to be very sure of my facts. My body was under par and unfortunately, there in the bush, I was attacked by a virus to which I had no immunity. I managed to carry on for the few days, but became quite unwell. On the way back to Sydney, I had to do a talk in the evening on constitutional homoeopathy, which is not always the easiest topic. In the middle of that talk, I started to shake. I managed to finish and, luckily, met up with Juliet and Hayley Mills. I had treated their father and mother and, as they were very concerned about me, they were of great help. It was lucky that God had sent a few angels to help me, as I felt absolutely awful. I saw a consultant in the hospital, who said that it was probably a viral attack from an unknown virus and I had pneumonia, which I'd had before. I was very ill indeed. He wanted to give me antibiotics, which I cannot take as I am allergic to them, and he said, 'Well, you cannot stay

in the hospital. Everybody has seen you today with your work on television and we can't have you dying in an Australian hospital!' That was, of course, true. I told him that I would go back to the hotel. That was a night I shall never forget. I prayed hard to God that I would not die in Australia and God answered my prayers. I used a whole bottle of Echinaforce that night and did all the cold and hot water treatments my grandmother taught me.

Early the next morning, the consultant came to my door. He said he had not slept all night as he was so worried about me and wondered how I was. I was in fact extremely ill. He helped me considerably and luckily I recovered, so that I was able to carry on with the rest of my work in Australia. By the next Saturday, when my niece and nephew came all the way down from Adelaide to see me, I was a bit better. Luckily, my wife wasn't informed, otherwise she would not have known what to do, but I told my niece and nephew that I was fine. However, the hospital consultant gave me a letter for my own doctor. Upon my return, I saw a doctor in Troon who was quite shocked and said immediately that I had to go to hospital. In the hospital, I met up with a very nice and understanding consultant who, in no uncertain terms, told me that I would need to spend a day in hospital as he believed I had developed diabetes. Indeed, the virus had attacked my pancreas and I had a blood sugar of 33 per cent (very high). I was given advice about injections, tablets and insulin, but I asked this doctor kindly if I could treat it myself and my blood sugar went from 33 to 16 per cent, and is now between 6 and 8 per cent (a good level is below 7 per cent). I have managed with my own remedies to keep this balanced, for which I am very grateful. Not that other people should do the same thing. With diabetes, it is very important to follow a consultant's instruction,

although a lot can be done to bring the blood sugar down through dietary management and alternative medicine.

My illness in Australia taught me a great lesson: the immune system is very important and when the three bodies are under threat, one should be very careful. So, temporarily, I had to reduce my workload, but happily I can now continue lecturing throughout this country and others as I did before, and still raise thousands and thousands of pounds for charity to help wherever I can.

I had some funny experiences in Australia too. I remember one evening, when I was lecturing to a large audience and feeling very tired, that there was a lady in the front row who never took her eyes off me all night. She was keen to speak to me afterwards and said that as I had worked so hard, would I go back to her house because she was very anxious to give me a colonic irrigation in order to make me feel a bit better! The only thing I wanted that night was to go to my hotel and then go straight to bed – certainly not to have a colonic irrigation! Sometimes it is very funny when you go around lecturing and remember the things that people ask you. Following another talk, one lady, after listening intently to my lecture, came to me and asked if my hair was its natural colour or if I used hair dye, as she hadn't noticed a single grey hair on my head during my lecture that evening. One can never forget some of these little stories.

Lecture tours, which I mainly do for charity, have been a great help to those in need throughout the world. The most unexpected situations sometimes arise during these tours. I remember in Northern Ireland, in a place called Warren Point, around 600 or 700 people were packed into a hall on a very stormy night and all the lights went out. I did the talk completely in darkness, managed to keep the audience cheery

and, shortly after the talk, when the lights went back on, there was great hilarity. When all these experiences are put in your path, it is a matter of trying to carry on and stand up and fight as best you can.

I had a great friend in Sir Stanley Matthews, and I always told him that he had feet like nobody else. His football talent was the gift given to him and during his last visit to me, I will never forget him saying, 'Whatever comes, keep going on.' That very often leads to victory and to the goal we want in life.

☙ CHAPTER THIRTEEN ☙

The Media – Friend or Foe?

While I was staying in the state of Indiana once, I was awakened very early one morning by the sound of a cock crowing. When, in the glory of that early morning, I looked out of the window and saw fields and fields without a soul, the sound of that cock crowing made me think of yet another full day of being with the media, for the strength of the media is indeed as powerful as the sound of that cock crowing far afield. Years after lectures and interviews on radio and television programmes, questions often come back to me: 'Why did you say this?' or 'When did you say that?'

One day, I was travelling by plane through three states of America, and was engaged in lectures, radio and television work. In the evening, I had a wonderful experience, as my friend, Roy Smalling, had hired a car to give me a fantastic surprise – or so I thought. He told me we were going to a place called Fort Worth Stock Yards in the state of Texas and that I would be in for a great surprise. It was very late at night when, after a fairly long journey, I looked around and saw that the streets were covered in sand, cowboys were walking around and it looked like something from the books I had read as a

child. Roy eventually told me that this was the hotel. The horses were tied up against the wall outside. Everything appeared to be made of wood: when we went inside, the floors, ceilings and walls were all wooden and I thought, coming into the bar area, that it looked very rough. It all seemed like a dream after reading about places like this as a boy. It was quite an experience, but the surprise did not end there, and was something I shall not easily forget.

I was quite tired and, shortly after arriving, asked Roy if I could go to bed. Even my bedroom was all made of wood, including the toilet, but, although very simple, it had all the necessities. I was exhausted and fell into a deep sleep until, in the middle of the night, I awoke with a great shock. Two big eyes were staring right at me and, although it was dark, there was a glare in them that frightened me. So I thought I would use the ostrich policy of putting my head under the blankets and going back to sleep. However, my Dutch nature – which is very nosy – refused to let me get back to sleep and every time I peeked over the top of the blankets, all I could see were those big, shiny eyes. Eventually, I could not stand this any longer, so I put on the light – and then I laughed and laughed and laughed at what confronted me. The wooden shutters on the window were not closed very tightly. The moon had been shining through the slats of the shutters and directly into the eyes of a horse's head that was mounted on the wall; it was the reflected moonlight that was glaring down at me. It made me think that we are often afraid of things that are not there, and the power of the imagination can be very strong.

It is not always easy dealing with the media and one has to be very well trained in what can be said, which can be very daunting, especially in my line of work where there is so much criticism. Fear can be one's worst enemy and there is a very

fine line between what one can say and what one cannot.

❧ ❧ ❧

When Mr Collins from the well-known publishing and printing company was still alive, we spoke one day about various stories and he encouraged me to write some books. I told him I was not a writer, but he asked me just to tell my story, as it would be interesting enough for his company to print. He suggested that I should write about what I thought was the most prevalent health problem at that time. Well, at that particular time, I found that stress and nervous disorders were the most appropriate health problems to write about, not knowing that 20 years later these disorders would be even more widespread. I therefore embarked on my book *Stress and Nervous Disorders*, which is still one of the best-selling books. However, the Collins company did not publish it and I was lucky enough to be advised to speak to Mainstream, then the second biggest publisher in Scotland. When I arrived one afternoon at their office, the two owners, Bill Campbell and Peter MacKenzie, were present. They had a small room upstairs in the building, packed with books, notes and a desk full of papers. To be honest, when I saw the enormous bundles of papers there, I feared that they would not even look at my simple little book. However, Bill Campbell looked at the manuscript and handed it to Peter MacKenzie, and a discussion then followed between them. I was quite sure that, with my bad English and grammatical mistakes, they would not be interested. However, to my great surprise, luck was with me and they said they would give it a try. The book was printed, went on the market and was a success – and remains so to this day.

After my book was launched, the media became interested.

Steven Williams, a London publicist hired by Mainstream, arranged several interviews for me; one of which was with Gloria Hunniford. Gloria was not very keen on alternative medicine at that time, but we managed to persuade her to do an interview on Radio 2. That was in 1982. The interview went well and Gloria often relates stories about my funny voice and the way I formulated my sentences. It made her smile and the public liked it. The programme was such a success that the BBC decided to do further interviews and, as it was a great way to reach out to the public, the publishers were very keen that I contributed to these programmes once a month or even once a fortnight. Those programmes became very influential and were listened to by millions of people. The letters we received provided clear evidence that listeners wanted to know more about alternative medicine and, from 1982 until 1992, I participated in these programmes. Nowadays, I appear with Gloria on *Open House* for television. Initially, Gloria was quite sceptical about alternative medicine, but I was pleased that she and her family became real converts to my work.

Other stations then started to get interested and one of the first presenters to come on the scene was a great friend of Gloria's, the very popular Sean Rafferty who broadcast on Radio 2 Belfast. Sean and I often recall the first programme we did together, when I got held up in traffic and we had no alternative but to conduct the programme by mobile telephone from the car until I arrived at the studio to continue the programme from there. It was the beginning of a long and fruitful relationship. The programmes became very popular in Northern Ireland, and for years I was able to give people simple advice on home remedies and ways of maintaining a healthier lifestyle. We had a great rapport and Sean often

helped me in my voluntary work when holding lectures for charities, by either opening events or helping to make these worthwhile. When the big choir, DEV, came over from Holland to do a concert for the Red Cross in Westminster in London, Sean introduced their music. That was a great media exercise, because DEV is very famous in Holland. We became a real pair of advisers and, after some time, I am sure that Sean knew what advice to give just as well as I did. It was great fun.

Because the programmes were so popular, the *Belfast Telegraph*, which is widely read throughout the world, became very interested and I wrote a weekly column there for many years, answering people's questions and giving them advice and guidance. I think it is very important that people receive guidance because they are often left in doubt, not knowing what to do and, for that reason, between Holland and Britain, I have written 40 books on the subject of health. Mainstream has been a tower of strength in this work and I shall be forever grateful for their guidance and assistance in doing this job. They have become real friends to me and have provided a backbone when writing the books.

Magazines became greatly interested and asked me to write for them – like *Woman's Realm*, *Woman's Weekly*, *Hello* magazine, *Top Santé*, *Here's Health*, *Ulster Tatler* – I could go on and on. The feedback from these magazines was great as lots of people wanted to know more about alternative medicine. The thirst for additional knowledge in this field became just as big here as it was in the United States.

I eventually had 22 radio programmes and about 4 television programmes. The impact of the features I did on *This Morning* with Richard and Judy was quite amazing. I participated in these programmes once a month for a number of years. Not only was it really great fun, but it also helped a lot of people

with their health problems. People asked me if I liked giving answers on television, probably because I was not used to it. I haven't even got a television in my own home as, with our busy lives, we need rest. Nevertheless, I realise that the power of the media is immeasurable and if it can help people and ease their suffering then it is a wonderful thing. I can well understand publishing companies' need for the media's help in order to sell books.

I sometimes feel sorry for people who are involved in this type of work because they are subjected to so much pressure and criticism that they need a nervous system made of iron and steel to withstand it. I remember once I was asked to do a tour of some of the old Dutch colonies – Curaçao, the Dutch Antilles, Aruba – all these places, including Guatemala. I was also asked to visit Bonaire, which was a quiet place. The beaches were white, the sand was glowing and the peace was almost heavenly. There, in that lonely place, I found a bundle of television stars and broadcasters, who had discovered a little oasis there. My old friend, Adele Bloemendal, so well known by the Dutch public, said, 'Come and join us here, Jan. At long last, we can get some peace.'

Relaxation is very important. I meet so many stressed people who drink too much coffee to keep them going, and too much alcohol for relaxation. Their busy lifestyles can put their bodies under enormous strain and it is comforting to know that they can sometimes find a place where they can rest and relax completely.

Anything that one does incorrectly can lead to big problems. I clearly remember on one of the programmes speaking about certain foods that are not good for certain illnesses, and trying to exclude certain foods from the daily diet that might be causing allergic reactions, or too much

acidity or alkalinity in the body. Balance is very important. With rheumatoid arthritis and psoriasis, I often suggest eating nothing from the pig. This almost led to legal action from the British pig breeders, as I was attacking the pig publicly by stating that it was not good for people. They wanted to take action against me but, on the programme, I said that, although the pig was a very nice animal, in some cases it was not good for people's health. So I managed to get out of that.

Some broadcasters were absolute masters, like Alison Brown from Radio Lancashire who, in only half an hour, managed to ask 40 questions. A lot of skill is needed in the making of these programmes to keep the broadcasters on the right side of the law, while still answering questions from the listeners as well as they can. Most of the programmes are done via the ISDN line, so I don't always need to travel. One programme I dearly loved and personally took part in for a long time was that of Radio Kent. Barbara Sturgeon, not only a very eloquent broadcaster but also a great personality, made it tremendous fun and the people she worked with were absolutely wonderful. Peter Rule, my PR agent, and I always looked forward to that trip and the fun we had.

It really makes me smile to think back to the sort of questions that I was asked. As I have a great affinity with animals, at one point we landed up with real animal programmes and on one programme – which I shall never forget – people came to the studio with their cats and dogs and all their problems when they knew I was there and the management had to tell me that I was not allowed to see anybody there as, again, it looked like a surgery.

Another experience that comes to my mind was on the *Gerry*

Kelly Show in Belfast, which I did regularly. On the show there was an entertainer called May McFetteridge, a transvestite. May entertains the public wonderfully and he is a very nice man but, funnily enough, when he is dressed up he looks just like a real woman. On the programme, Gerry asked me if I would do some iridology. I looked in the eyes of quite a number of people, told them what could be wrong and, to their astonishment, they said that that was exactly what was wrong with them. So, in front of the public, May asked me what I found wrong with her. When I looked deep into her eyes, I told her that I saw that she wasn't really a woman, but actually a man. This caused great hilarity and those shows have been a great success.

It is a wonderful thing when one can provide evidence of the work one is doing. For years, I prepared columns in the *Daily Record* and the questions were quite amazing, but I was happy when I switched over to the *Sunday Post*. I had not realised that that paper was so powerful. Today, the *Sunday Post* is still one of the biggest papers. I think it is so much loved and admired throughout the world because of its simplicity and the fact that they write the truth and do not sensationalise situations. The editor who does the pages with me, Carolyn Smeaton, has great knowledge as a layperson of the whole field of alternative medicine, and she often improves on the articles I have been writing.

The media is very powerful. Over the years that I have written and broadcast in this field, I have received a great deal of feedback. One day, I was at Olympia in London where I spoke four times to absolutely packed halls with large groups of journalists. One of the journalists said to me, 'Remember when you started here that there was only a handful of people. Now there are hundreds and hundreds, if not thousands, who

have become followers.' It was wonderful when one of the visitors stood up and said, 'I watched you on *This Morning* with Richard and Judy for many years and was initially completely against alternative medicine, but you converted me and thank God you did, because I now feel like a new person and have a new lease of life.'

When people try to criticise and say there is nothing in alternative medicine, I ask them to just try it – try it for three to six months and then see how you feel. I know that most people will then come back and say that they have a new lease of life. Every broadcaster has his own style of working and yet, sometimes, one is surprised. A broadcaster from Canada comes to mind. With all my personal experience, I would say that he is the best broadcaster I have ever worked with. He was very well versed in his subject, had a great rapport with people, and yet, the last time I was over in Canada, he had gone. The station didn't want his services any more. It often saddens me when I have worked with people for so long, that they suddenly disappear, often without a word of thanks from their employers and colleagues. The world of the media is very cold and is one that I personally would not like to be part of. Today is everything, tomorrow is nothing. The media can also be extremely hard and twist words. They can take certain phrases from a book without giving the whole picture, thereby giving people the wrong impression, or they can attack you with something that, taken in the context it was written, probably has a totally different meaning but, given a twist, comes out incorrectly and can have repercussions. National stations, international stations – they all have their attractions and their listeners, but a lot depends on how the message comes across.

I once did a talk for a big group of ladies. There was a large

turnout of journalists and I could see that the man who was to introduce me was very tired and probably bored. He told everybody that I was a great speaker and that he, for one, had looked forward to the talks I would be giving that day and knew that the rest of the audience would find them very interesting. After I started my talk, he fell into a deep sleep and, when his colleagues woke him after I had finished an hour later, he stood up telling everybody what a wonderful talk it had been. That is typical of my experience of the media.

I get an enormous number of letters following television programmes. One letter from a lady really surprised me when she wrote to say that she was absolutely glued to her television when I was on – but, instead of listening to what I was saying, she was more interested in my wavy hair! She asked me if I wore a wig as, at my age, she felt I couldn't have such dark, healthy-looking hair. I was sorry to hear this because I neither have a wig nor colour my hair, and would have been happier if she had been more interested in the topic I was discussing than in my hair!

Another story I will never forget concerned my great friend, Len Allan. I will write about him in more depth in the next chapter, but I had given a talk on the radio, after which there was time set aside for questions. A lady phoned up and told of her child who had weeping ears, which I know is very, very difficult. Being over-enthusiastic, I said to her that it was quite easily solved. I said she could do such and such, and I even said that she *should* do such and such. I got a phone call from my friend, Len, who had listened to the programme and was highly shocked that I had advised this lady that she must give her child this and that. He had been in practice for over 50 years and told me that in all that time he had never said to any patient 'you *must* do this and that', because it is forbidden by

law. He was sitting shaking in his chair listening to the radio, wondering what the nation must be thinking of what I was saying. That, again, was a great lesson.

People constantly ask me to keep in touch and, especially after seeing my newspaper articles and hearing my radio or television programmes, want to be kept informed on the developments of complementary medicine. I am very pleased that, after a lot of hard work, I have established our own magazine, which comes out four times a year and is called *In Touch*. The circulation has grown fast and it is much easier to get my messages across to people this way. No matter where I am throughout the world, when I see new developments I am so very anxious to share this information with my patients and ex-patients. *In Touch* has made this possible.

The *Health Check* television programme in Belfast has become very popular. It is quite astonishing that enormous numbers of people want to be on this programme, either for advice or for diagnosis. The variation of problems is so amazing that the viewers are glued to their screens to see what advice I will give.

Thinking about the power of the media reminded me of a programme I was on in 1991 with Mrs Logie Baird, who was then in her nineties and whose husband invented television. She said that if her husband could have envisaged how people would become addicted to their television screens and what an enormous part it would play in the lives of families, he would have been ashamed. People who have an addiction to television should realise that it is not good for their eyes. To watch television once in a while is fine, but not – as one patient told me she did – switch the television on in the morning and switch it off at night when you go to bed. That is dangerous.

However, I am happy that the media has spread the

message. For that reason, I cooperate with them so that people in this country have freedom of choice, whatever treatment they decide to pursue.

When the first alternative health conferences were held in this country, the media regarded them as some sort of quackery, whereas nowadays these conferences are of huge interest to the public. I was happy that the magazine, *Here's Health*, which has a wonderful team, asked me to give out awards to the best companies from different countries that have produced the finest products in this field. There were a lot of awards and what pleased me was that companies who would never have looked at alternative medicine previously now, thankfully, have received the awards that I presented to them. Giant companies like Boots, Waitrose, Sainsbury, Tesco and Marks & Spencer were next to small companies who have done their best to pioneer this market and who have overtaken the giant companies when they realised the huge potential that was there to be tapped. It was with a certain pride that I gave out those well-deserved awards for the kind of products that we see on the market today, which are well promoted and so well received by the public. It was also a great privilege for Dr Vogel's company, Bioforce, to receive the top award. I just wish that Dr Vogel could have been alive to see how much his products are revered in this country and that his lifetime's devotion has been so worthwhile. Dr Vogel and others who have followed in his footsteps have worked with an open vision to give freedom of choice to the public. Personally, this is also my mission and I am grateful to the media for their help, but this interest must start with oneself. Even if I have to preach it on the streets, I am happy to work for an honest cause to help alleviate human suffering.

Some time ago, when the alternative medicine exhibition in Edinburgh took place, I arrived to make two afternoon speeches. My talks there are always packed. We were told that there was no electricity and the public was not allowed to go into the building. Everybody was so disappointed and upset, until I suggested that we should go to Rose Street, behind the Assembly Rooms in George Street, where there were benches. I managed to find a big box and a loudspeaker and, in front of hundreds of people, conducted my lectures in the street. It was a glorious Sunday afternoon and, as more and more people came to listen, it was wonderful to be able to preach the message of health there in the streets.

One day, when I was speaking at a big yoga seminar, the hall was so warm that I advised the audience that we should go out onto the street. Hundreds of people joined us and we had great fun. Afterwards, the press wrote about this fantastic interest in the different forms of alternative medicine.

Sometimes the public itself is a great form of media. I was very encouraged by a small incident. On her way to my clinic in Troon was the wife of a very well-known doctor in Edinburgh. She had with her a consultant from one of the hospitals in Edinburgh. Both the consultant and the doctor (my patient's husband) were very against alternative medicine. In fact, they laughed about it. My patient, who was in great despair, had been improving and, reluctantly, her husband had to accept this. He said, 'Whatever this man is doing, just keep doing it.' That was the reason he agreed to bring his wife back to me. So, on that sunny afternoon, they were all on their way to visit my clinic, and also to see Royal Troon golf course. When they were near Lanark, they got a flat tyre. They were in the middle of nowhere, but managed to spot a farm. They went up to it and the farmer who

answered the door asked them what they wanted. They asked if they could use his telephone. He said, 'Absolutely not. When I let people into this house to use the phone before, they stole some of my belongings. You will just have to go.' They told the farmer that they were on their way to Troon because the lady in the car was quite ill and had to see a doctor there. His face lit up as he asked, 'Is that the Dutch doctor?'

The gentleman said, 'Yes, I believe he is Dutch.'

The farmer asked, 'Is he small, and is his name Jan de Vries?' They said that was correct. The farmer then told them that they could use the phone for nothing. He added, 'That man cured my back some years ago and I have never looked back. Please use the phone.'

When young practitioners have just started in practice and don't have enough patients, I have often encouraged them to keep going and hold on. If they are good and know what they are doing, they will reach their goal. I have often repeated to them the words of Sir Stanley Matthews who said, 'Keep going, fight back and you will be victorious.'

CHAPTER FOURTEEN

Pioneers and Fighters for Truth and Freedom

This chapter is about the pioneers of alternative medicine and, although I will write about the ones I have known personally, it would also be good to mention a few who, throughout the world, have done their best to open people's eyes to something that has become very valuable today.

Samuel Hahneman, the founder of homoeopathy, had three principles that he preached to diagnose a problem: look at the image of a person, look at the life force in a person and don't just treat the problem, but also treat the cause of the problem. A lot of the people we know from history, such as Lust, Kneipp, Benjamin, Priestnitz, Bircher Benner, Vogel, Lindlahr and, later on, Thomson, Leaf, Jay, and many others who have gone before, pioneered different fields, and also laid the groundwork for a wonderful team who have carried on from them and are working just as hard today for justice, truth and freedom for what has now become complementary medicine.

When I came to this country 42 years ago, my very first visit was to the Kingston Clinic in Edinburgh. I met old Mr Thomson, who had very extreme ideas on nature cures. He treated patients with the four naturopathic principles, which

are treating with food, water, air and a little manipulation and massage. Hydrotherapy was very important. Without doubt, the patients I spoke to were all quite happy. I was also pleased to speak to Mr Thomson a bit about the past and the difficulties he encountered with his views on medicine then. I asked him how high the cancer rate was in Scotland. He told me that it was 1 in 18 to 20 at that time, whereas today it is 1 in 3, with bowel cancer being the highest in the world – which is an enormous increase over that 40-year period. When I spoke to him about the past, he told me how Stanley Leaf, John Jay and he started a practice together in Hanover Street, and about the different paths they eventually took. First of all, Stanley Leaf went to England and later formed a very well-known clinic of nature cure called Champneys, while Thomson formed Kingston, the beautiful estate where so many people found peace and rest. Nowadays Champneys is run more as a beauty farm. Later on, John Jay, who was the assistant at Kingston, went to Ayr. His story is quite intriguing.

John was an excellent practitioner who had many followers, until something happened in his life that made his beliefs become very extreme; although he wrote intelligently about his views on medicine and how people could help themselves towards better health. My third daughter, Tertia, is a medical herbalist. She often saw a man who looked like a tramp walking barefoot in the streets of Ayr, with an old bike and a little basket, rummaging through dustbins for lettuce or cabbage leaves, and she became intrigued. Tertia had no idea who this man was, and one day asked him why he had so much seaweed in his basket. He told her he used it for his potato growing, which he did in a small field. He was homeless and living in the open air, but had small plots of land where he ate greenery and potatoes grown in seaweed. She asked him why

he was so extreme in his views and if she could help him in any way. He asked her who she was, and she said her name was Tertia, the daughter of Jan de Vries, a naturopath. He shook his head and said to Tertia, 'I am a naturopath. Your father is not. He practises homoeopathy, herbalism and acupuncture but that is not the same as nature cure.' He was quite right, as a naturopath only uses the four methods that I mentioned. This man, a tramp, turned out to be John Jay.

Tertia got quite interested in talking to him and asked him what had happened. He told her a bit of his story. She then said, 'My father would love to meet you,' and he replied, 'I would love to meet your father.' Arrangements were made that he would come to Auchenkyle on the Sunday afternoon. Just before he arrived, I had a phone call from the police to say that a tramp had been seen around Auchenkyle and to ask if I was aware of this. I said that I was, and that I had been expecting that particular gentleman. Before he arrived, Tertia had warned me to put plenty of air fresheners in the room and, indeed, when he arrived, you could see that he was living like a tramp. We had a most interesting talk and I learned a lot about the British forefathers of natural medicine whom he had studied and worked with – people like Semple, of whom I had never heard, but who had such a wonderful history. My knowledge of the forefathers of British nature cure was very limited. I was also intrigued by this man himself because, although he was in his nineties, he still had some teeth and looked in perfect health. I asked him what had happened, but he did not want to talk about it. However, I later learned that his wife, who was a doctor, had left him and, because of the shock, he had become a bit peculiar. He insisted that people's immune systems would greatly improve if they lived in the open air and ate the greens from the field. This was actually

what he did. Even on the coldest nights, he would sleep in the streets, still barefoot, and lived not only on the greens of the field, but also on the vegetable leaves he found in people's dustbins. He could not stand the wastage he found. He would rummage through bins for any vegetable leaves he could find, wash them in seawater and then eat them. Although his views were very extreme, his knowledge of naturopathy conveyed in his writing made very interesting reading. I wanted to stay friendly with him and help him with his work, but this became impossible as unfortunately he became absolutely obsessed with my daughter Tertia, who had to be very hard on him. From that day, he did not come near us again, so there was not much we could do about it. Not long after that, he wrote quite a big article in the local newspapers about interference with drinking water and the use of herbicides, pesticides and fertilisers. Unfortunately, when John died, nobody really knew what age he was, but I knew from his history that, when we met him, he must have been well into his nineties.

This was something I saw in Holland too; where some of the old fathers of naturopathy became very extreme and no longer had both feet on the ground. There were also some who became quite vindictive and dogmatic. Today, when I think of several practitioners I have known, I am grateful to them for the knowledge they have left us and the work they did to make naturopathy and the different methods of homoeopathy, acupuncture and other forms of alternative medicine better known. As I have often said, it is high time that orthodox medicine (yang) joined alternative medicine (yin) in a great marriage of complementary medicine. Apart from everything else, they are both trying to ease human suffering. I often think of Dr Vogel who did so much to bring this nearer to the masses and to help people understand his work. Although

some of the work of the pioneers was understood, sadly they were sometimes hampered by the 'powers that be', who didn't want their message to succeed.

I often think of the day when, after heavy lecturing at a medical conference in Switzerland, I went to my hotel room, ready to go to bed, when I heard a knock on the door. Outside stood an old Japanese gentleman who had lectured that day, with his wife. He asked if he could talk to me. When I let him into my room, he told me a wonderful story. Although he wasn't a believer, or even religious, his wife, who was a Roman Catholic, had persuaded him to go to Lourdes. He explained that he had an inoperative throat tumour and he went to Lourdes where he drank plenty of the water. When he researched, he found that germanium (a very potent mineral) was in high concentration in the water there and he felt, although this water might be blessed, that it was the germanium that had such a great effect on him. He tested this on all kinds of illnesses and diseases, but found it most effective in the treatment of cancer and degenerative diseases. After all, it had cured his throat cancer and he was therefore so enthusiastic that he wanted to share his knowledge with others. Unfortunately, he was unable to as the media reacted badly to his findings. Today, it is still very difficult to get germanium, especially in some countries, and the complicated research required means it will take some time before this wonderful remedy can be proven to help. It sometimes takes a battle to overcome negative attitudes in the media, which can be, as I said in the previous chapter, either a friend or foe.

Dr Hans Moolenburgh found this out when he almost lost his battle against fluoride being added to drinking water. He had so much scientific evidence on self-medication and the harm that fluoride could have in drinking water that he

attacked the Dutch government and did what he could to keep it out of the drinking water. He nearly lost his battle, until he was allowed to appear on television, when he managed to convince the entire Dutch public that adding fluoride to their water could be harmful. It was not only because he was a doctor, but also because he had the scientific evidence to prove the harm that fluoride could do if it was added to the water supply. He had a great following and therefore won his fight and managed to get fluoride banned from drinking water. He too, even today, is a fighter for freedom and feels that every person should have freedom of choice in the way that they are treated.

Dr Benthem Oosterhuis fought for the freedom of homoeopathy and won. In a great example, he showed the Dutch people what the combination of good dietary management and homoeopathy could do for them. He was living proof of this as, even when he was over 100, he still bicycled. Together with him, I set up the Alternative Food and Drug Administration which controlled a lot of the foods that were not up to our standard.

I attended the last seminar of Keith Lamont, who died shortly afterwards. Although he was old and not very fit, it was still his wish to share a few of his ideas with those who were interested. Not only did I learn a lot from him at his last seminar about things that interested me and methods that I still use today but, above all, I admired his interest and enthusiasm demonstrated by the fact he still wanted to share some of his findings with his younger colleagues after being in practice for so many years. When I looked at him that day, I wondered how long he would still be here and how much it would take out of him to spend a day teaching, but his desire for others to understand the enormous wisdom that he had

gathered over the years was so strong. I am grateful to people whom I have known, as teachers and as lecturers, over the years who have now passed away.

Apart from Dr Vogel, I have given seminars myself to get his message across to others. One of my best teachers, who also became one of my best friends, was Dr Len Allan. Len wrote five very valuable books on his work as an osteopath and acupuncturist and, as a man who knew a great deal about nutrition, gathered knowledge from all over the world and incorporated this into his books. Today I am adding to and editing the great work that he did, in a book I will call *Dr Len Allan's Almanac*. This will be a valuable book for young practitioners of the future and will be a treasure for them to have in their practices. I often think of the amazing results that Len achieved and the value of his teachings and the knowledge that he gathered from all over the world. Even when I was in Australia and went into a doctor's surgery, I saw his chart, which he had put together so cleverly, in one of the consulting rooms. I was struck by what this man had taught me and I have been privileged to learn all the methods he practised for years. I followed many of his seminars and these were of great benefit to me. He did a wonderful job and had much success where others failed, and I am very grateful today that I have been able to help people because of what he taught me.

A very well-known lady from Belfast came to me. She had a problem with her coccyx and her husband told me that he had spent over £4,500 trying to help his wife with this problem, but to no avail. On one particular Saturday, I carried out one of Len's procedures on her coccyx and, on the Monday, she phoned to say that the tremendous pain and suffering she had endured had gone. Her husband returned two weeks later and asked me if I could take him on as a

patient. This was one of the wonderful things I learned from Len, and something that I shall always be grateful for.

I am always disappointed when people who have taught so many and to whom we should be so grateful have been forgotten. Unfortunately, Len's mind went, and when I visited him not long before he died, I asked his wife, Doris, if some of the old students ever visited him and she said no, that I was the only one. Even though he was very ill, he still recognised me and the smile on his face reminded me of the many good jokes that he would tell us during his valuable lectures.

I think of Gonstead in the United States and his neuromuscular techniques and chiro techniques, especially for the adjustment of a hiatus hernia. When I think of the many people I have saved from operations by performing this adjustment, I am so grateful for the opportunity of attending some of his seminars and for the knowledge that he shared with us while I was over there.

I developed a tremendous friendship with Dr Willem Khoe, who used to be a surgeon but became interested in osteopathic techniques. He taught me many of these, in particular a jaw adjustment that only he could do. He showed me the procedure probably about 50 times before I mastered it, and I have since helped many people who have had problems with speaking, singing, sciatica, neuralgia and headaches, after the jaw has been put out of place during treatment by the dentist. I remember the tremendous interest that arose when I carried out this technique on television on *This Morning*, after which many people contacted me. A tremendous amount of expert help and knowledge was needed to perfect this technique, and a lot of research went into finding out the best and easiest ways to adjust the jaw. After all, it is vitally important to get the balance right. As is often said, when the wheel in a watch

stops, the whole watch is no use, or if a ship is laden too much on one side, it will capsize – the same also happens with the human body, where harmony and balance is absolutely necessary.

In the summer of 1971, I had a letter from a professor in London. He said in his letter, 'I am a caller in the wilderness, nobody listens to me and yet I controlled my multiple sclerosis.' I wrote back and said that I had treated multiple sclerosis for many years but never had great results and would love to meet him. He wrote back and invited me to go and see him. Shortly afterwards, I went to visit him in Hampstead in London. I rang the doorbell and heard somebody walking very quickly down the stairs, when the door was opened by Professor Roger MacDougall. Very cheerily, he said, 'Come upstairs with me.' He took me into his lounge and told me his story. At a certain age, after he had written the scripts for two very well-known films, he developed multiple sclerosis. It was diagnosed as progressive and, a few years later, he was trapped in a wheelchair and was nearly blind.

One day, when he sat there feeling miserable, he said to himself, 'Roger, your name is up in Glasgow University as one of their most clever pupils. You have not used your brain.' He had heard that in Holland during the war there was no Crohn's disease, coeliac disease, and very little diverticulitis or diverticulosis. Looking into this, he discovered that the diet in Holland at that time was low in gluten, and people ate quite a lot of fruit, vegetables, nuts and natural foods. He decided to remove gluten from his daily diet and take some extra vitamins, and see what happened. After some months, he felt he had a bit more power in his legs. He looked again at his diet to see if he could improve it further and decided to cut out most dairy products, along with refined sugar. He then

reviewed his vitamin intake and added evening primrose. Four and a half years later, his sight came back, he could walk again and he returned to normal.

As Roger was telling me this story, his neurologist arrived. Roger had asked him to come while I was there to confirm to me that he was a fully diagnosed MS patient and that he was not in remission. We had a very interesting talk. Afterwards I had to see some Dutch patients in the Hilton Hotel Park Lane. Roger offered to walk with me and I was very surprised when we walked the length of Piccadilly Lane from Piccadilly Circus, talking about his wonderful findings and the possibilities of helping so many people. He was fully convinced that people with MS could improve their condition if they adhered to the diet completely and took extra vitamins, minerals and trace elements (especially the B vitamins) to supplement it, and evening primrose. From that day on, I adapted his diet for use in my clinic and have, over the years, treated hundreds of MS patients. I became very friendly with him and his ex-wife, with whom he was still friendly, and who came to stay with us in our residential clinic, where we nursed her and helped with her problems. We met up many times after that, lecturing together at universities, to doctors, and abroad. His programme has been of great benefit, not only for people suffering from MS, but also for schizophrenics and patients with autism. Something that he did develop was the great desire to help his fellow human beings who were in the same boat as he was. It is impossible to cure multiple sclerosis, but you can control it – I have seen evidence of this many times.

With great admiration, I remember Dr Kelley, a dentist who was dying of cancer. Dr Kelley and I had a lot in common. We were always digging for the truth and he felt, like me, that the

answers to many problems can be found by searching seriously. He used to say, and I will never forget this, that searching for answers is like the story in the bible of the man who had a field. This man knew there was treasure hidden somewhere in the field, but he had to dig for it and make every effort to find that treasure. Once he found it, he knew how much he could do with it. We both felt we had found treasure in the course of our work, and that it could not be taken from us. Dr Kelley had to find how to look after his body when it was stricken with cancer. This was a huge shock to him, and certain emotional traumas that had happened during his life had made his cancer worse. He looked for an answer, and found that cancer was a metabolic disease. He started to study it and found that certain vitamins, minerals and trace elements were of benefit. He devised a naturopathic nutritional programme, very cleverly computerised, and worked out which remedies would help. This was a great achievement and he shared his knowledge with others, such as the Mexican doctors Gonzalez and Gonzalez. Others studied his methods and continued researching the illness, and many people were helped.

Others expounded great ideas, like Harold Manner and Virginia Livingston, who worked on a system that was vitally important in helping alleviate suffering. It takes courage to make a stand; I clearly remember a banquet held after a big conference, when I sat next to Ann Wigmore, the author of the book *Be Your Own Doctor*. While everybody else enjoyed the delicious food, she sat there with a plate of wheatgrass. She was the healthiest girl in the world and had found treasure in the use of wheatgrass and natural living. She helped cancer and AIDS patients and had great results, and it was a terrible shock when I heard that she had died in a house fire. She did so much for others – I would have liked her to have had a much longer life.

I think of Dr Heede's methods; he was instrumental in my writing the books *10 Golden Rules for Good Health* and *Healing in the 21st Century*. I think also of the Max Gerson Institute, continuing the work of Dr Max Gerson, which is practised even better today, with all the discoveries that have taken place in this big field of medicine. Many pioneers were involved in these discoveries and research, and many had the guts to tackle the industry.

I remember a great friend in America who had a wonderful farm. After a conference, she invited me to go there, and on the way bought two chickens from one of the large battery chicken factories. The chickens were big, and had been injected with water (amongst other things) to increase their weight. When we arrived at the laboratory, she did a blood test. The test showed that the blood contained cancerous cells in one of the chickens and pre-cancerous cells in the other. She then took a chicken from her own farm and did a blood test on it – the results were normal.

I learned a lot from the pioneers of complementary medicine I have known. Many have now gone, but they left a legacy of truth and freedom of choice. They did their best to work for causes that are still relevant today. There is the example of Wakefield, who had doubts about the MMR vaccination and had the guts to stand up and fight against it, while awaiting the evidence of the effects of the injection. A few times during my 45 years in practice, I too have had to fight for the freedom of choice in this matter, so that these inoculations can be administered in three parts and not in one combined shot. The little body that gets that shot is very often not able to cope with it. There is also the example of Dr Yehudi Gordon, who fought and won the right for pregnant women to take an active part in the birth of their

babies, completely against the wishes of the establishment and after a long fight.

Every day, information trickles in from researchers. The pioneers in medicine are the ones who stand up in the fight against an establishment which finds change hard to accept; for example the New Zealand doctor who fought for the acceptance of the helicobactor pylori and the ones who fought for the official recognition of candida albicans, a yeast parasite (the establishment often said there was not such a thing). Then there are the doctors who fought for the recognition of ME by the World Health Organisation, who diagnosed this wrongly by stating it was a disease of the nervous system – it is in fact a disease of the immune system. Our immunity is something that we all have to protect.

Dr Moerman, a Dutchman, had to fight after he lost his only daughter to the monstrous disease of cancer. He thought long and hard and, looking outside at his pigeons, thought, 'Why don't my pigeons have cancer – why don't *any* pigeons ever have cancer?' He looked at the lifestyle of the pigeons and what they were eating and, after a lot of research, came to the strange conclusion that it must be their diet. Like Dr Kelley, he recognised the importance of dietary management, as cancer is a metabolic disease. The Moerman diet became very well known, although the battle by the establishment to keep him quiet was fierce. There were a lot of powers at work that didn't like Moerman's ideas, but he kept fighting. When my friend Hans Moolenburg became one of the ten Moerman doctors in Holland, I remembered the expression 'the truth will set you free'. Moerman's work became more widely known and he continued to fight for truth and freedom until finally the Dutch government recognised and accepted his ideas.

Nobody wanted to know when Dr Shamsuddin, an Indian

doctor I recently met in London, recognised that inositol (IP6), a protein found in the minute inner wall of a rice grain, could block the growth of cancer cells and was a great boost to the immune system. I was very impressed with the work that Dr Shamsuddin did over the years in cancer research and with IP6. He has done so much for cancer research; I was very happy to talk to him into the small hours of the night. He worked so hard to discover what he did and I was very pleased when an oncologist wrote to me, having monitored some of his cancer patients, stating how impressed he was by the help the patients had received from IP6. He was hungry for more information and wanted to know all about it. Many of the pioneers in this area had the vision to work in a field that was virtually unknown, but learned how to control cancer cells. It is amazing to think that the minute part each of these doctors played can have such an impact in the war against cancer cells. Cancer is warfare between two armies of cells – regenerative and degenerative. Even with the aid of chemotherapy or radiotherapy, the army of regenerative cells must be as strong as possible to fight the cancer and, therefore, immunity has a very important part to play.

Today we should be grateful to the pioneers. When I started in this field in Britain almost 35 years ago, I can think of a few people who helped me in the fight for health. Many have brought naturopathy into focus today, like Roger Newman Turner, whom I call the father of naturopathy, and Joe Goodman, whom I call the father of acupuncture. Joe worked with Rose Neil, a very good friend of mine who also fought very hard to bring acupuncture to the fore in this country. Many other people also did their best to bring these methods into the public eye, and contributed to their popularity today.

My grandmother wisely taught me the secrets of nature

when I was a young boy and, in her own way, talked to me about the importance of a balance of energy. My mother also fought for the truth. When she died, I sadly lost a good and true friend. My father lost his old set ideas and became an example and, as he often said, 'The best thing in life you can do is to be a good example.' There are too many people for me to mention here whom I have met in my lifetime and who have fought for freedom and truth, and despite a lot of opposition kept working for this, which was so necessary to improve our understanding.

When I think of that little army fighting against the big army of the establishment, I know that they all understood the biblical expression: 'Where there is no vision, the people perish.' (Proverbs 29:18)

The Other Side of the Coin

After the many years of criticism, abuse and insults of various kinds, the sun is rising above the horizon of what is now called complementary medicine. When I look back over the years, at the difficulties Dr Vogel and I faced when we opened the first naturopathic clinic in Holland, the jealousies and misunderstandings, and the way practitioners of alternative medicine were provoked by the establishment and media, I am grateful that those pioneering years have passed.

I have received many letters, some bigoted, others very nasty, threatening me with legal action and sometimes advising me to stop practising alternative medicine altogether. Now there is more understanding and a wider view of what is meant by complementary medicine: using both principles of medicine, alternative and orthodox, to help and assist in alleviating human suffering.

Now we can finally contemplate the integration of alternative medicine into a complementary system. Many times I wondered if this would ever come about, especially when doctors lowered themselves to very public attacks on my work. Some doctors even went as far as placing articles in the local

paper expressing their concern when I opened an X-ray centre above our health food store, claiming this had caused the whole street to be contaminated by radiation – this was complete and utter nonsense, as the X-ray centre was fitted by the best people in Scotland, HA West in Edinburgh. Every care was taken to ensure that it was not only totally safe for the patients, but for the whole area in general. As well as this, the benefit to patients of quick diagnosis was tremendous. It was an excellent service and I still value the support of all the neighbours who laughed at the doctors' scaremongering tactics. When the Inspector of Health was called in to investigate the complaint, he verified that the job had been done well, and, as he was leaving, I asked him to tell the worried doctor who initiated this inspection to stop such low attacks and become better informed before he sent articles to the local newspapers.

On another occasion, at a local Rotary Club lunchtime meeting, I happened to mention that I had been asked to lecture to doctors and nurses at a local hospital. During the course of that afternoon, I was told that the hospital had been instructed to cancel the lecture because some individuals in the medical field had heard me saying that I was giving this talk – yet another insult.

At a lecture I once gave on natural medicine, the person who gave the vote of thanks claimed that there was nothing of value in health foods or health food medicine. However, that very afternoon, the very same person was seen snooping around in one of our health food stores to find exactly the products I had been talking about earlier in order to sell them in his chemist's shop! No wonder, after so many years, I have a real laugh about it all. When I think of the many people who criticised me and sent awful letters (which have since become treasures to me), I realise just how childish this kind of behaviour was.

People like that, who are full of their own self-importance and criticise alternative medicine without knowing anything about it, will go into history as being totally foolish in their objections.

At one point, I remember, I wanted to join a local club and two doctors fiercely objected to my membership. It was as if I was insignificant because I practised alternative medicine. One would never believe that such behaviour could exist, and it is pitiful. Those people showed themselves up as being very narrow-minded.

I will say that, although I could stand up to that behaviour, at times I felt sorry for my children, who attended local schools and were sometimes looked upon as odd because their father practised a very strange form of medicine – as it was then seen. Even when my children were older and some of them went into orthodox forms of medicine, I was conscious that, while they were growing up, I was not seen as a valued member of society. In those days, alternative medicine was often seen as quackery. When I was joined by my first proper assistant, a well-qualified physiotherapist, I remember her father angrily told her that she was not to work for a foreign quack. Little did he know that I had an orthodox training behind me, training which to this day is recognised by the health authorities.

It is interesting to witness the developments that have taken place in alternative medicine over the years. When I think of the times I have been asked by hospitals to open units for acupuncture, the many lectures I have given to postgraduates at universities and the university talks and lectures I have given, I say, 'Well, isn't it amazing that we now have the same situation as Copernicus had in his day and age, when he expressed his views on the solar system and was made out to be a fool!'

Society has changed considerably over time and sometimes it is necessary to have an open mind to gain knowledge. Nowadays, after my early struggle, I see the other side of the coin; I receive complimentary letters from hospitals and, not so long ago, an oncologist from a research unit almost begged me to go to the hospital to give a lecture on a few of the methods I had been working with. He fully recognised that there had been positive results from the use of alternative medicine. I have also received letters from universities I have lectured at, and have often said that I am open to any discussion.

Not long ago I had a conversation with Prince Charles, and we both admired the way in which alternative medicine has become a very recognised part of our society. He was quite surprised that, during the time I have built up the ten clinics, orthodox doctors and alternative practitioners have come to work so well together in a complementary system that is beneficial to patients. I have often found a lot of understanding among the members of the Royal Family whom I have treated, as they have often looked into alternative medicine and researched it more fully than many other people.

Personally, I don't really care what people think of me – what I am concerned about is my patients, and I want the very best for them. Whichever method is used, my main desire is for them to get better. Orthodox, alternative or complementary – it doesn't matter, as long as the patients benefit, although I am happy that there is so much recognition and approval of the field of alternative medicine today.

I have been honoured with many titles over the years, but, to avoid causing confusion, I have never really used them. In all fairness though, it is with a certain amount of pride that I am able to use the title of 'Dr', as I was privileged to be

awarded an honorary title in medicine from the most excellent International Academy Pax Mundi. I have never used my doctor's title, however, nor have I made much of the many decorations I have received, such as the Order de la Croix de Jerusalem, the Order of St John, the Order of St Brigitte of Sweden, the Creation Order and the Royal Knights of Justice Award, or the many certificates from my own profession, fellowships, etc. I could go on and on. I am very grateful for these, and very proud to have received them. These honours and the recognition they demonstrate are all very well, but the most important reward for me is that I have the approval of my Creator, who gives me the strength to carry out my daily work and helps me to try and make people better – that, for me, is the most important part of my life and as long as I have that I am happy. God's love is of the greatest importance, and it has also shielded me from the many dangerous situations I have been in during my life. It protected me from being shot in the Second World War, from danger when I was in a hijacked plane, from being involved in a severe traffic accident on the busiest road between The Hague and Rotterdam, from being a victim in a train crash when around 140 people were killed, from being nearly killed by a nasty virus in the bush in Australia, and from a traffic accident where amazingly my wife, Joyce, and I were saved from a monstrous lorry that stopped just centimetres from our little Peugeot. These are some of God's wonders, for which I am grateful, because I know that I am protected by the Creator who wants me to continue in my work to help the suffering.

Sometimes it helps to look back. When things were really difficult, because of jealousy and opposition from others in my own profession, I felt powerless against those who wished to destroy me because of my success. I phoned my mother to ask

her what I should do in this situation. She said to me that you reap what you sow: 'This will not hurt you, but it will hurt those who do it. It is the only justice in life.' When I think back over the years of what has happened to those people, I now know that she was right. As she said, you get out of life what you put into it. The only justice in life is that one gets back what one gives, whether good or bad.

❦ ❦ ❦

While I was sitting talking to a patient one day, my faithful housekeeper knocked on the door and handed me a letter. It stated on the envelope that the letter had to be opened immediately upon receipt and she therefore felt she had to disturb me to give me it. When I read it, I got a bit of a shock. I managed to finish my conversation with the patient, but afterwards read it again immediately. The letter actually said that I had to pay £50,000 at a certain place within two hours, otherwise Auchenkyle and everything in it would be blown up. The blackmailer said he had written the letter because I had not treated his mother and sister to his satisfaction. There was no signature, but it sounded serious enough. He said he would phone and tell me where to go to hand over the money. I immediately phoned the police, who put me in contact with the CID. They took the letter very seriously and immediately phoned me back, as they believed this was the same character who had written similar letters to several other people, and who was only out to extort money. Indeed, it was serious enough that they felt I should act on it and do exactly what he said, if he was the same man, as one or two people had been victims of this particular person. So, when he phoned, I cooperated with him fully. He wanted me to go to a particular

telephone box with a black bag containing the £50,000. I told him that I could not possibly get away, but would send my manageress, and she would meet him at the specified time and place to hand over the bag. He was happy enough with this arrangement at the time, but then started to make threatening phone calls every 15 to 20 minutes, which made the staff in Auchenkyle very nervous. When I asked my manageress if she was prepared to help, she said she had absolutely no objection to doing this and, because she was one of my best friends, I knew I could rely on her.

So she went, followed by plain-clothes police officers. When she arrived, there was a little man in the telephone box who, becoming suspicious at the various cars driving around, ran away and disappeared. The police couldn't catch him. Everybody was very nervous – nobody had a clue who or where he was. A search started. The police manned our phones all day and kept their eyes open for anything out of the ordinary. At that time, I had a very clever assistant who helped me with patients and she told me she had seen a blue van in the road next to the estate, with a man in it, writing something. The police were obviously very interested in that information, and they jumped into their car and sped away. Within half an hour, they returned with the happy news that they had caught him. They had been misled by others who had mistakenly thought they had seen the man in a yellow car, but when they found out it was a blue van they managed to track him down.

It was a very sad situation because the case would have to go to court, and it would be a very lengthy process as there were about 10 or 12 other charges against the man. I was very nervous because I could ill afford the time involved to sit through all those court cases. Luckily, I was one of the first to

go to court. I had never been involved with the police before, nor had I ever been involved in a court case in my life, and I was also slightly nervous that the mother and the sister would hold what had happened against me.

The day before the court case, my wife, Joyce, took me for a drive. It was a lovely summer's day, and I can vividly remember coming across one of the nicest views in the world, at Tighnabruaich, at a high point looking out over the Kyles of Bute, and thinking it was heaven. There was a little plaque on the point where we stood which said 'I will lift up mine eyes unto the hills, from whence cometh my help.' (Psalms 121:1)

I felt very calm the next day when I went to court because I had nothing to hide, although the defendant's solicitor was very rough on me, and I always said if I ever needed a lawyer to defend a case for me, I would ask him because he almost made me feel guilty even though I had done nothing wrong. However, I had a very strong case and was touched when the mother and sister came to give evidence. To my amazement, they were completely on my side, and told the court how much I had done for them. That was a wonderful experience. The court case lasted a few days, after which time the jury came to the decision that the accused was guilty.

It is wonderful to have friends in life. Two old ladies whom I knew sat through the entire court case and it was reassuring to know that they were behind me and praying for me, so that this case came to a satisfactory conclusion. It was comforting to feel protected by a higher power who has the last word in everything.

⅋ ⅋ ⅋

It is often encouraging to see how conversations develop. I was once talking to Pat Kenny, the famous Irish broadcaster, and another doctor who criticised homoeopathy. He said there was absolutely no proof of its efficacy. I told him that a ten-year study had shown that the lowest potency in homoeopathy had affected mucous cells when tested, and it was proven that there was a scientific aspect to homoeopathy. The doctor muttered, and I will never forget Pat saying, 'Well, whatever, you can never argue with results.' This I have often said. Although homoeopathy and some forms of alternative medicine are often criticised, if the results are obvious, it doesn't matter what works, or how, just as long as it does. At many meetings, when certain subjects such as life energy and balancing energy are introduced, some professors put their hands up in the air and say, 'Prove it, show us and let's see how it works.' This is sometimes difficult, but over the years I have often put the ball back in their court. It causes a bit of a laugh, but nevertheless makes the point, when I ask them to explain to me how conception works. There are things that we can explain scientifically, and there are things we cannot. There are some areas where we have only scraped the surface but although they may sometimes be difficult to prove, they all have a purpose in this life-fulfilling plan.

This brings me to one of my experiences of how orthodox and alternative medicine can work successfully in a complementary system, where benefits can be seen. Back in the days when I did interviews with Gloria Hunniford, a little girl, aged seven, came to me with her mother. I saw them both very briefly in the George Hotel in London, where I had a short conversation with them. The girl impressed me by the way she so graciously accepted her very serious illness, which was thought to be an inoperable brain tumour. She had all the

symptoms – drooping eyes and a very deteriorated state – and I could see that her mother was fighting hard for her only and beautiful little daughter. She asked for some advice as the surgeon wanted to operate. When she mentioned to the surgeon that they were coming to see me, he encouraged them to do so and also said that he would cooperate in every way possible with anything I suggested. I told the mother that, by law, only the oncologist was allowed to treat her child's cancerous state, and he would do this in conjunction with the neurosurgeon. I could only help boost her immune system in order that her little body would have the strength to cope with what she had to face, and back up the operation with treatment afterwards. The girl's father was in the service of Her Majesty the Queen, and he was in agreement with my treating his child, so I took the girl into my care, helping to boost her immunity, and strengthening her for all that she had to go through. I also gave her some remedies which helped to balance her white and red blood cells. Basically, that was how I treated her and, after the operation had taken place and I introduced some other remedies, the surgeon was very impressed with the speed of the healing process. He asked me what I thought of using laser treatment to divide the remaining particles left over in the brain, and I agreed that this should be done. Overall, the treatment of this lovely little girl was very successful and it is with pride that I see her now, as a young woman, just how well she has done, and how grateful she is for all the help she received.

The laser equipment being used in that particular hospital was becoming obsolete. The girl's mother wanted to raise enough money to buy a new laser to help other patients in their treatment. She asked for my cooperation which, of course, I gave, and then she told me there would be a big

concert in Her Majesty's Guards' Chapel in London, which the girl's father would supervise. She was adamant that she wanted me to be there, but I told the mother that I was not very keen on these big occasions and, as I would be in London working all that day, it would be difficult for me to be there on time and also I would not be able to attend in formal evening wear. She still felt that I should be there. After work, I went to my favourite accommodation in London, the YMCA, where I always stayed because it was so central. The mother somehow managed to trace me and begged me to come, saying that her daughter thought the evening would not be complete if I was not there. I was very upset, as I felt I would not be properly dressed for this special occasion. Eventually, I agreed that I would go, but said I would sit behind a pillar. I managed to take a double-decker to Buckingham Palace but unfortunately, on leaving the bus, a piece of metal that was sticking out tore a hole in my trousers and I felt absolutely awful. I managed to get some tape to temporarily repair them and carried on to the Guards' Chapel. When I arrived, the guards who were at the gate asked me who I was and I was told to wait. The father of my little patient arrived with the guards and, flanked by them, I was marched into the chapel. Whatever happened, I did not want a fuss. Nevertheless, I was given a place of honour. I felt absolutely terrible as I saw the seats being filled by many of the Royal Family, our Prime Minister, other ministers, people of great importance and celebrities. Further attention was focused on me when my name was mentioned, and also when the little girl publicly gave the surgeon and me a kiss to thank us for all we had done. That was an honour I shall never forget but, nonetheless, I was quite upset and embarrassed by the whole situation. At the same time, I was very happy that complementary medicine had

received so much recognition that evening, and that it had benefited my little patient so much. After the concert, when I met several members of the Royal Family and celebrities, I was very encouraged to see the other side of the coin and the growing recognition for something that potentially could develop into a real integration as, after all, the aim of both principles is to help the sick.

* * *

Some time ago, a series of articles appeared in *The Sunday Times*, written by Dr Michael Gearin-Tosh. The articles appeared following a book he had written called *Living Proof: A Medical Mutiny*. When I read the first article, I saw my name mentioned. Since that time, the book has swamped the British market and has been read by many people. After the publication of these articles in *The Sunday Times*, people throughout Britain talked of this spellbinding book that revealed the whole truth of the treatment of the doctor's cancer. It is a book that has been an eye-opener for many, but especially for the medical profession.

I remember this Oxford doctor and lecturer arriving in my clinic in the north of London. He had no appointment, so I did not have much time to spare him. When I saw him I could tell immediately that he had problems, but as there was no taste in my mouth and nothing visible in his aura, I knew that he was not dying, and could therefore put his mind at rest when he told me that he had a short time to live as he had quite an aggressive cancer. He was a very nice man who I could see was not only very well educated, but also had a wisdom that stretched further than I had thought. He was the first man since I went into practice to suspect that I had an

extra sense of intuition that assisted me in my work, and he wrote about this. After many years of being repeatedly asked what my secrets were I decided, now that Dr Michael Gearin-Tosh had let the cat out of the bag, to reveal some of them in this autobiography, which I had been planning to write for some time. It is thanks to him that I have now written this book. I felt the time had come for me to share my little stories, probably due to the fact that I have been in practice for nearly 45 years.

Michael Gearin-Tosh wrote that, when he was on his way home after seeing me, his friend who accompanied him asked him what he thought about me. He told his friend that my eyes had been focusing on him for a whole minute and that I had said to him, 'One look at you and I know you do not need chemotherapy.' During the drive back home, his friend told him about doctors with extra senses in his country of Kurdistan. They could sense a patient's magnetic field and aura. He suggested that perhaps I had this gift, or that I might have been trained. Well, I had no training in this. I discovered my gift at the age of four, have worked with it all my life and never usually talk about it. That is why Michael Gearin-Tosh was the first person to suspect. I have humbly accepted this gift of intuition and premonition as a great help to me in treating patients.

Throughout his book, Michael talks about my extra sense. He wonders if it played a part when he had a breakthrough with his cancer through the wonderful Chinese breathing exercise I taught him, writing: 'Did he pierce some inner world . . . Whatever, I feel I can climb a mountain.' Everybody has a gift, but it is as I wrote earlier – a treasure in a big field that one has to dig for, find, cherish and use. I personally feel, as I have said before, that it has a lot to do with breathing.

When a baby is born, it becomes a living soul, breathing for life through its nostrils and becoming a living being. 'The Lord God formed man of the dust of the ground, and breathed into his nostrils the breath of life; and man became a living soul.' (Genesis 2:7) This wonderful breath of life that God gave became the soul of man, alive and in harmony with its creation. Our health depends, however, on how we use that breathing. While an asthmatic breathes from the chest, a very relaxed person breathes from under the navel. This greatly affects the harmony between yin and yang, the streams of life and death, and correct breathing can bring relaxation and calm. We see with illness and disease that the way in which we breathe plays a very important part. This has a tremendous influence on the endocrine system (in other words the seven endocrine glands) and is in tune with the cosmos, thus making it very valuable. Other capabilities we do not know about may have been unlocked by individuals who have learned to be in contact with the cosmos and can use their gifts in prayer and meditation. These are very important tools which can be used to nurture this particular extra sense, as they can influence the electromagnetic field which emanates from every one of us. Everybody is surrounded by colours that should be in harmony and can be found reflected back in the eye retina. That is why iridology often plays an important part as an accessory in diagnosing patients.

Being in harmony with nature means being in harmony with one's Creator, and that means obeying the laws of nature, which will bring peace. One of the reasons that Michael Gearin-Tosh's treatment was such a success was that he perfected the Chinese breathing exercise, which I explained to him was necessary to bring new life into his system and also to overcome the negative thoughts surrounding his condition. He understood what it

meant to unlock these positive powers within himself in order to overcome the negative powers. After all, as I have said before, cancer is a war between the two armies of cells and the more the army of regenerative cells is strengthened, the more chance of life there is. We also see this influence when visualisation techniques are practised frequently, even when one has come to the end of the road. Positive will always win over negative. I often tell patients to look at the battery of a car, where there is a positive and a negative. Right in the middle of that battery is a zone where nothing happens, which we call the neutral zone. This is also the case with people, and through the neutral zone, we have to use powerful methods to add positive energy and, in so doing, help strengthen the immune system. For almost 45 years, I have been looking after patients and have found that if I can unlock a patient's negative attitude by the use of just a positive word or thought, that patient is halfway to recovery. In this warfare, where there are all kinds of diseases, you need to keep fighting, hold on, and victory will come. There are tremendous powers in everybody that are unused or never discovered and which are of great value in making life worthwhile, by simply opening oneself to what the future holds. With this higher power and guidance, we can accept the saying I have used before: 'It is not in man that walketh to direct his steps.' (Jeremiah 10:23)

Sometimes things happen that we don't expect – we might have intuitions or premonitions, but life is always full of surprises. Bad things can happen in life, but if we look at the positive things, they often make up for it. The years of fighting for my beliefs in my profession have not been easy and yet the positive things that have happened during this time have given me the encouragement to carry on and made me realise how good it is to be alive. To be able to breathe in the powers of

nature, to look all around at the wonderful things that have been established and then, without warning, to get a little pat on the back from an unexpected source, makes all my efforts seem worthwhile and are great reasons to fight on.

⚬ ⚬ ⚬

When I was nearing completion of this book, a registered letter arrived for me. It was from one of the well-known universities in Scotland. The letter stated that because of all my good work and the several breakthroughs I have had, as well as my teaching (especially for students) and writings, Queen Margaret's University College in Edinburgh had granted me a Professorship in Complementary Medicine. It was an honour I did not expect, but humbly accepted, because I love young people and am encouraged by those who have the foresight to see what they can do with their lives, especially in helping others. I am grateful for the life I have still got and I am extremely happy with the amount of work that I do. In order to share the knowledge I have gained over the years from working closely with so many great masters in this field, and from my experience of working with patients, I hope to establish at Queen Margaret's University College the biggest library on complementary medicine, so that young people can have access to the works of the masters I have learnt from, as well as my own works. I will be donating the books I have inherited and the ones I have written myself. It is also hoped that the lectures I give will be of great benefit to students in the future when helping others. It is with the greatest enthusiasm that I will start this challenging job and give my very best to the students.

As for the future, I look forward to writing part two of my autobiography!

192

OTHER TITLES BY THE SAME AUTHOR

BY APPOINTMENT ONLY SERIES
Arthritis, Rheumatism and Psoriasis
Asthma and Bronchitis
Cancer and Leukaemia
Heart and Blood Circulatory Problems
Migraine and Epilepsy
Do Miracles Exist?
Multiple Sclerosis
Neck and Back Problems
New Developments for MS Sufferers
Realistic Weight Control
Skin Diseases
Stomach and Bowel Disorders
Traditional Home and Herbal Remedies
Viruses, Allergies and the Immune System

NATURE'S GIFT SERIES
Air – The Breath of Life
Body Energy
Food
Water – Healer or Poison?

WELL WOMAN SERIES
Menstrual and Pre-Menstrual Tension
Pregnancy and Childbirth
Mother and Child

JAN DE VRIES HEALTHCARE SERIES
How to Live a Healthy Life
Questions and Answers on Family Health
The Five Senses
Inner Harmony
Healing in the 21st Century

NATURE'S BEST SERIES
10 Golden Rules for Good Health

THE JAN DE VRIES PHARMACY GUIDEBOOK SERIES
The Pharmacy Guide to Herbal Remedies

ALSO BY THE SAME AUTHOR
Life Without Arthritis – The Maori Way
Who's Next?

A STEP AT A TIME

LIMERICK CITY LIB.